Everyday Practices for Better Living

Tracey Howarth Tomlinson

2QT Limited (Publishing)

2QT Limited (Publishing)
Settle
North Yorkshire
BD24 9RH
United Kingdom

Copyright © Tracey Howarth Tomlinson 2020

The right of Tracey Howarth Tomlinson to be identified as author of this work has been asserted by her in accordance with the Copyright, Designs and Patents Act 1988

All rights reserved. This book is sold subject to the condition that no part of this book is to be reproduced, in any shape or form. Or by way of trade, stored in a retrieval system or transmitted in any form or by any means, electronic, mechanical, photocopying, recording, be lent, re-sold, hired out or otherwise circulated in any form of binding or cover other than that in which it is published and without a similar condition, including this condition being imposed on the subsequent purchaser, without prior permission of the copyright holder.

Cover and internal graphic images: shutterstock.com and iStock

Printed by IngramSparks UK Limited

A CIP catalogue record for this book is available from the British Library

ISBN 978-1-913071-86-8

Acknowledgements

This book is dedicated to all the spiritual and meditation teachers who have inspired me with their wisdom over the years. I thank you.

Also for my sons, Conor and Joshua, and for my husband Mark, who has supported me throughout.

Get in Touch:
Website and blog: angelreis.com
Facebook: Tracey Howarth Tomlinson Author
Instagram: @tracey_rachel

Medical Disclaimer

The information provided in this book is designed to provide helpful information and not intended to replace any medical advice nor does it offer any diagnosis or treatment for medical conditions. The publisher and author are not responsible for any specific health or allergy needs that may require medical supervision and are not liable for any damages or negative consequences from any treatment, action, application or preparation, to any person reading or following the information in this book.

Therefore if you have any health/mental health problems, or if you are currently taking medications of any sort, you should consult your doctor or equivalent health professional prior to undertaking any of the suggestions in this book. Reading this book does not establish a therapist-patient relationship.

References are provided for informational purposes only and do not constitute endorsement of any websites or other sources. Readers should be aware that the websites listed in this book may change.

Contents

Acknowledgements	3
Medical Disclaimer	5
Introduction	13
Chapter One - Meditation	17
Fight or Flight Response	18
Recognising Stress	18
How Meditation and Mindfulness Can Help	21
Meditation Space	23
Preparing a Meditation Space	25
Furnishing Your Space	27
Meditation Ideas to Get You Started	28
Meditation Summary	35
Chapter Two - Connecting with Inner Awareness	36
Focused Awareness	39
Developing Space Between Thoughts	40
Mindfulness on the Go	41
Chapter Three - Raising Your Spiritual Vibration	45
Vibrational Fields	46
Diet	48
Exercise	49
Other Ways to Raise Your Energies	50
Using Visualisation to Strengthen and Protect the Auric Field	52
Ways to Find Calm	53
Smudging	54

The Path of Least Resistance and Raising Vibrations	55
Writing and Using Positive Affirmations	57

Chapter Four - Kakeibo – The Art of Money Mindfulness — 60

Kakeibo Journal — 62

Chapter Five - The Abundance Mindset — 65

Abundance Mindset Summary — 67

Chapter Six - Finding Your Life's Purpose — 69

A State of Allowing — 70
Allowing Changes — 71
Soul's Purpose Summary — 77

Chapter Seven - The Importance of Gratitude — 80

Expressing Gratitude — 81
Gratitude Is an Element of Success — 83
Keep a Gratitude Journal — 86

Chapter Eight - The Power of Positivity — 88

Practise Thinking More Positively — 89
Positive Speech — 90
Establish a Morning Routine — 91
See the Good in All Situations — 92
Forgive Others — 93
Building a New Blueprint — 95
Positive Affirmations — 95
Moving Through Fear — 97

Chapter Nine - Goal Setting — 100

- Goal Setting Steps — 102
- Visualising Goals — 103
- Creating a Vision Board — 104
- Making Your Vision Board — 105

Chapter Ten - Journaling — 107

- The Medium — 109
- Language — 109
- Time — 110
- Privacy — 110
- Reflection — 110

Chapter Eleven - Harmonious Relationships — 112

- Problems in Communication — 113
- Resolving Conflict — 114
- Relationships and the Law of Attraction — 116
- To Love Oneself is to Connect to the Divine — 118

Chapter Twelve - Stopping Repetitive Thoughts — 120

- Coping Strategies — 121

Chapter Thirteen - The Power of Prayer — 125

- Personal Form of Prayers — 126
- Belief in Prayer — 127
- Prayers for Guidance — 128

Chapter Fourteen - Decluttering – Mind and Life — 130

- Clutter Can Be Stressful — 130
- Ways to Start Decluttering — 132

Some Strategies　　　　　　　　　　　　　　134
　　Decluttering the Mind　　　　　　　　　　　135

Chapter Fifteen - The Miracle of Early Mornings　　137

　　My Miracle Morning　　　　　　　　　　　140
　　Miracle Morning Practices　　　　　　　　143

Chapter Sixteen - Coping in Challenging Times　　148

　　Coping Strategies for Stressful Times　　　153

Appendices　　　　　　　　　　　　　　　　　156

Introduction

If you have found this book then it is likely that you are searching for inner peace in an ever more fast-paced, frantic world. The price we pay for this faster, more technologically advanced world is stress. This book came about after my own searching for the answers to life's deep questions. Why here? Why now? Why me?

The exercises and ideas contained within this text are to help you on your own personal journey of self-discovery.

On my journey, searching for inner peace and for the answers to these questions, I discovered ways of letting go of the anxiety that tainted my life so inextricably and the illness that it caused. Stress manifested itself in many forms within my mind and my body. I have searched in many ways over the years to live a more meaningful, balanced life, and this book was created to share the things I have discovered along the way.

It was once thought that people were born either happy or unhappy: you were born into this world with your lot and you had to just make do with it for the rest of your life. Thankfully, that thinking has now changed. Over the years modern thinkers and scientists have developed ways of overcoming an unhappy state of mind and altering the course of your mindset to one of inner peace and happiness. Indeed, many of the techniques of mindfulness and meditation have been formed from the Eastern philosophies that have been known to scholars for millennia.

It is seemingly increasingly difficult to find inner peace in a world that moves at an incredibly fast pace and where we are continually bombarded with choices, information and stimuli. This book aims to present ideas and exercises to achieve more calmness and a state of mindfulness in all areas, even finances, through mindfulness with money (by using a Japanese budgeting method known as kakeibo). It is hoped that the ideas in this book will help you in achieving a higher perspective, an inner awareness, and that ultimately you will find a greater sense of inner peace.

All the practices in this book are ones that I have personally implemented in my life to help me become a more peaceful and productive person. I'm not perfect. Far from it. However, I carry out most of the strategies presented in this book daily, to put my mindset on a smoother course: one that is more positive, focused and aligned.

Some days will be better than others, but with a more positive and calm mindset, great things can be achieved and difficulties negotiated in a more rounded way.

In this text, I draw on some concepts that have been explored in my previous work, and also on the wisdom of my favourite authors, such as the late Wayne Dyer, Eckhart Tolle and Joseph Murphy, among others. Many of these writers are part of the new thought movement. These writers brought about new concepts of living by examining the benefits of positive thinking, the law of attraction, creative visualisation and personal power, thereby unlocking the secrets to a better life. All these themes are explored throughout the text.

The ideas, concepts and exercises explored in the text offer ways in which mindfulness, positive thinking and the law of attraction can be applied to daily life, in order to live a more mindful, peaceful, balanced and yet productive life.

Many similar themes run through the book, so in some chapters some themes may be touched on but then revisited and looked at in depth later. There is a reason for this. Firstly, it is to introduce concepts in certain chapters, particularly if the reader chooses to read some chapters but not others. Secondly, I have found through my years of learning and study that there are common themes and strategies used in various concepts, particularly in relation to journaling, meditation and mindfulness, and the use of positive affirmations. Indeed, the chapter on the miracle of mornings uses many of the strategies that have been looked at in depth in the preceding chapters.

Meditation and mindfulness are key to changing your mindset as a whole. Meditation calms and clarifies the mind, removes the brain fog that clouds thinking and puts the practitioner on a path of greater awareness of the self and the world around them. Many therapists use meditation and visualisation to tap into the inner core of a person's being. These techniques can be used to release past hurts, alleviate repetitive thinking, help with anxiety, reduce stress and, overall, improve your health, both mental and physical. I'm witness to that: through meditation and changing my mindset I got through some of the darkest times in my life. This is why I'm so passionate about meditation and the other topics explored in the text.

One common theme presented in the text is journaling.

I suggest you buy a journal specifically for the task. Of course, you may wish to do it digitally, but I feel that a physical journal is much better for organising thoughts and ideas and for creative flow. Journaling is a wonderful tool in sorting out feelings and ideas, and can help tap into creative solutions to problems too. If you are struggling with a particular situation that is giving you problems, writing about it can help you come to terms with it and can get any anger, angst or frustration out on to paper rather than storing it up.

Another common theme is organisational skills. The most successful people I know are highly organised. They are people who are up early, who have structured lives and who are focused, constantly setting goals. Their success doesn't come at the expense of others. They don't constantly moan, nor do they belittle others. They live in a constant state of harmony, focused intention and gratitude for everything that they have.

Life is a journey, not a destination. You have the power within you to create the life you truly want. We have within us the ability to transcend the illusion of life to create our own reality, one greater than we could ever think possible.

We are all born with unlimited potential. Choose your thoughts the same way you would choose your clothes each day. This book is about changing your mindset and becoming the best version of you.

Chapter One

Meditation

So, why meditate? Many people meditate as a way of reducing stress, of clearing the mind, of reducing anxiety, and as a way of improving mood, concentration and clarity of thought. Don't get me wrong. Meditation and sitting in stillness are acquired skills. It can be testing to try and still the mind while in the act of meditation. However, the benefits that meditation can give make the regular commitment to meditation practice worthwhile. Meditation can have a positive impact on your health and well-being.

The regular practice of sitting quietly in meditation can assist in making those connections to the inner peace that exists within the recesses of the mind. Sitting quietly and focusing on the breath are crucial to stilling the mind and connecting to the subconscious part of the self that holds higher wisdom and creative ideas. Meditation is a doorway to connecting to the guidance and inner wisdom which exist within our subconscious mind that you would not normally access in the fast-paced lives we live today. That is, unless we learn to still the mind and body in periods of quiet reflection and contemplation.

Meditation is very useful in helping reverse the effects of stress, in addition to calming the mind and the emotions.

In today's fast-paced world, many demands can be put on our daily personal and working lives, especially if high standards and high expectations are part of your lifestyle. We can end up living very full and often stressful lives, with little time to focus on our own sense of self and well-being. While a little stress can be OK, in fact some stress can be beneficial, continued stress can make us emotionally and/or physically sick. Prolonged stress can affect our bodies, moods and behaviour, and can ultimately lead to many health problems, both physical and emotional.

Fight or Flight Response

When under threat the glands in the body release certain hormones so that we can prepare to fight or run away from danger. This in turn causes reactions in the body, making the heart beat faster.

This response is part of our ancestral make-up and been present in humans since the time when we had to run from wild animals or were faced with real danger, at which point the choice was taken to either to stay and fight or flee to safety. The physiological and psychological response to stress enables the body to react. In today's society, because of the fast pace of life and the stresses and strains of daily living, some people find that this response is provoked not only at times of real danger but also when they are faced with what they perceive as stressful situations. An example of this is when faced with an imminent physical danger such as being attacked by another person or a more psychological threat such as preparing to give an important speech or presentation.

Phobias are examples of perceived threat, where the fight or flight response is triggered. For example, a fear of spiders may be to some people an irrational fear, but to the person who experiences the phobia it is a real fear, whereby the body may respond with an increase in heart rate and an increase in the rate of respiration. In more severe cases this can in turn lead to a panic attack.

Recognising Stress

When you begin to recognise the symptoms and triggers, strategies can be explored such as ways in which you can find calmness and help the body relax. New ways can be developed to help individuals deal with their reactions to stress and stressful situations.

At many times in my life I had quite severe panic attacks. This was in part my body's reaction to stress: part of my own fight or flight response. Some of the responses I had could be triggered by simple things such as being the only customer in a store and having an irrational fear that I was being constantly watched.

The reaction that I had highlights that it was not the actual event that caused the stress. Rather, it was the overrunning thoughts building in my head and the stories that I was telling myself which began to lead to the emotional upset that then led to my physical response: a panic attack. Events like this would end up ruining my whole day. It felt like a vicious circle: anxiety would well up in me again whenever I thought about these types of stress-inducing events and I would get worked up thinking about them, and then another panic attack would happen.

In effect I was repeating these stories in my head over and over again.

The body can experience many healing effects from the processes of meditation, such as a lowering of the heart rate and slower breathing patterns, a reduction in the production of stress hormones, the stabilisation of blood pressure and, over time, a stronger immune system.

One study showed that after completing a meditation retreat of six days, there were significant reductions in depressive symptoms and stress, and this continued for ten months after the retreat ended for some participants (Gilbert et al, *Journal of Alternative and Complementary Medicine*, May 2014).

There are various neural oscillations or brainwaves active in our brain during various states of brain activity. During meditation the brainwaves alter to a distinctive alpha pattern.

During our waking state, when we are alert and when we are engaged in a problem-solving activity or making decisions, the brain is dominated by beta waves.

Alpha brainwaves are created typically when we are daydreaming or consciously engaging in mindfulness or meditation. Interestingly, alpha brainwaves are also stimulated when participating in aerobic exercise. Many studies have been conducted which suggest that the stimulation of these brainwaves is linked to enhanced creative processes and the reduction of symptoms of depression. Alpha brainwaves may also aid memory, reduce pain and alleviate stress. While meditating one can experience enhanced mental awareness while simultaneously feeling deep relaxation.

People who regularly meditate can move into this mode

at will. This allows them to counter stress more efficiently, helps lower the blood pressure and combats muscle pain. Regular meditation can help calm the mind and emotions. It also is excellent for relieving symptoms of anxiety and can help lower blood pressure (Bergland, *Alpha Brain Waves Boost Creativity and Reduce Depression*, 2015).

Stress creates a fog over our mind and hinders the ability to see or perceive situations with clarity, and it also clouds our judgement. When we get stressed, we just can't think straight. Meditation and mindfulness can help to lift this mind fog. Subsequently, better decisions can be made, clarity of thought can be achieved, we can see situations as they really are, and we can react to them in a calm and positive manner.

How Meditation and Mindfulness Can Help

Mindfulness and meditation stimulate creative processes. When your mind and body are calm you can access your intuition and your imagination with greater ease. This is where your hopes, dreams and creativity reside. When you can access this source of creativity and wisdom you will find that you will be able to attract what you want in life more easily. You will also be clearer about what you want to attract and want to create in your life.

Meditation and mindfulness can assist greatly in personal development, but you do not have to live the life of a hermit or a Buddhist monk to achieve the level of calmness and well-being that the practice brings. A little every day can go a long way. With practice and perseverance meditation and mindfulness can change your life for the better in a relatively short space of time. Consistency is key.

My own meditation practice started many years ago. I would – and still do – meditate at the same time each day, and would try to aim for about twenty minutes at a time. Some days it would be minutes, some days half an hour. So long as I completed my meditation practice, I noticed that I felt much better. Today, many years later, I can meditate for hours at a time.

I noticed that after a period of time, the panic attacks I suffered from began to subside. When I did feel a panic attack sweeping over me, I used my meditation breathing techniques to calm down. After a while, my panic attacks began to disappear.

Meditation is an important part of my daily practice. I meditate for at least twenty minutes daily, in the morning, before I get ready for work to prepare my day ahead. Daily meditation has helped me regain my self-confidence and restore balance and harmony to my life. Prior to discovering meditation and mindfulness I suffered constant anxiety and periods of debilitating depression. By taking the time to still my mind I discovered an inner well of peace and stillness that I never experienced before. My life began to run more smoothly and, although I still experienced some challenges in life, my meditation practice helped me to deal with those challenges in a calm and more measured manner.

During my meditation practice I am able to tap into the creative processes which naturally reside within my subconscious mind that help in my gaining creative solutions to my problems. Through practising my daily meditation the beginning of my day started to evolve into a whole new, less erratic and less stressful way, which would continue throughout the day. Added to this, I found that I became more able to handle stressful events in a measured manner, events that previously might have sent me into a spiral of angst, panic and despair, with no idea what to do next.

While that is good for me and fits in with my schedule, you will need to find your own routine to fit meditation practice into your own life. You may want to meditate in the evening when the kids have gone to bed, and you may not even be able to meditate for a full twenty minutes. Start doing little and often, and continue to build on your practice to find what is right for you.

You do not need to live the life of a recluse to achieve the calmness and well-being that meditation can bring. Meditation is, after all, an acquired skill that you need to persevere with.

Meditating at the same time each day can help incorporate your practice into your daily routine and develop a regular meditation habit. There are also many apps that can be downloaded onto your phone to help you develop your practice and keep focus. Having a designated meditation space can also help.

Meditation Space

In the early days, when I started to work on my meditation routine, I didn't have a room or space that I could call my own. Living with a small family in a packed terraced house, I just didn't have the luxury of claiming a personalised space just for me. What I did do, however, was to claim a small space in my bedroom, on my side of the bed. There, I had a shelf on which I put some crystals, a Buddha sitting in the lotus position and an incense burner. That was my space, my little portion of the house where I could regularly take time out to meditate and calm my senses and my mind after a busy, full-on day.

At roughly the same time each evening, when the children were in bed and the day's chores were done, I completed my practice. Once I had meditated in this space a few times, the energy changed, so much so that every time I entered my meditation space, a sense of relaxation and peace would automatically envelop me. When the children got older and we moved to a new house I claimed a small box room as my own and filled it with all the things that help create a peaceful and spiritual environment. I do still, however, meditate regularly on my side of the bed as well as in my little room. Old habits die hard. Habits though, cultivate regular meditation practice.

Once you have chosen a space where you can meditate you may wish to prepare it in such a way that it enhances your meditation experience. Whether it is a spare room that you can claim for yourself, or simply a small space within an area that you can call your own, it is nice to prepare it in such a way that it reflects your spiritual practice.

When you meditate regularly in one chosen space, the energy of the area will change. Your mind and senses will tune into the sense of stillness and peace you achieve when you use the same space each day for your practice. You will consistently associate that space with the purpose you use it for.

Preparing a Meditation Space

We have dedicated spaces in our homes: a place to eat, a place to cook, a place to sleep. Why not have a dedicated place to meditate in? Your space could be in the corner of a room, a spare room in your house, a garden shed, a conservatory or even a spacious cupboard under the stairs.

A place for conducting your meditation practice in doesn't have to be big. As mentioned previously, when I began my practice, my meditation space was at the side of my bed with a shelf, upon which I put items to help me focus my intention.

Once you have chosen your space, make it yours and remind others in the house that this is your space, especially if you have a busy household. Keep your space tidy, clean and free from dust. If it is in the corner of a room, make sure that the whole room is uncluttered and clean. Also think of the energy in the room. Does the atmosphere, the energy of the room, feel ambient, peaceful? If not, think about how you can change it. You may need to decorate. Choose pastel and neutral shades, and steer clear of intense, bold colour schemes. You can cleanse your room energetically by using a bundle of sage (known as a smudge stick), a singing bowl or some tingshas.

The burning of herbs and oils in ritual cleansing is common to many cultures and can be found in shamanic rituals and in churches alike. The same can be said of sounding bells and other similar devices.

Smudging is the practice of burning a bundle of sage to clear spaces of negativity. Smudge sticks can be bought from any New Age store. The most common are variants of sage bundled together.

To smudge a space, light one end of the bundle and place it on a plate (you can use an abalone shell to catch the embers). Waft the smoke from the smudge stick with a feather fan or with your hand, holding the intention in your mind that by doing so you are cleansing the space of all negativity. Once this is done sufficiently, extinguish the smudge stick safely.

Smudging can be used to cleanse and purify spaces in the home to lift the energies. Smudging can also be used in the same way to cleanse objects such as crystals, which can be passed through the smoke to clear away any potential negative energies.

Alternatively, spaces can be cleared by using the power of sound. For this purpose, a singing bowl can be used, or some tingshas.

A singing bowl is a metal bowl (some are machined, some are hand-hammered) that makes a distinctive sound when rubbed on the outer rim with a wooden mallet. They exist in various sizes, and their size dictates the sound they make. Tingshas are small Tibetan cymbals that make a sound when struck together.

Any of these tools can be used to clear a space energetically. Just hold the intention in your mind that all negative energies are being dissipated, leaving only positive ones.

Arguments, negative behaviours, violent games and films can all leave an energetic imprint on an environment. You only need to bring to your mind how the atmosphere feels when you enter a space where an argument or fight has just taken place. By smudging or using sound any negative vibes in the environment can be energetically brushed away, leaving a positive, uplifted energy in its place.

Furnishing Your Space

Creating an inviting meditation space for you to use will assist in encouraging you to spend quality time meditating. Every person's home is their castle, so the saying goes. It is a place to retreat, a sanctuary, a place to go to get away from life's stress. It is a space in your home, however small, that you can devote to having that quality me time in. This is time that you can spend in quiet introspection and inner reflection, which should radiate those peaceful energies you seek.

The following items are suggestions about what you may wish to put in your meditation space.

If you have enough room, have a small table or a shelf to put objects on. These should be objects that inspire you. They can be crystals or carvings and statues, such as angels or Buddhas, and so on. Alternatively, invest in a cupboard to place items in, which can be opened when you are going to meditate. This is a popular practice in Eastern traditions, where the cupboard doors are opened to reveal a dedicated altar for when your meditation practice takes place. It also keeps your items safe and contained.

Have a nice chair, cushions or a beanbag to sit on. Some people like to sit upright in a chair while meditating, whereas some people prefer the floor on a cushion or beanbag. Make sure you decorate your space with items to inspire you, such as prints, tapestries and/or pictures of deities, saints or angels. Ensure that you have nice covers and soft furnishings and cushions. A touch of nature, such as a plant or flowers, adds a nice living element to any space. Other objects, in addition to crystals, may be special stones picked up during your travels, or feathers, shells, and so on. You may also include aromas such as essential oils in a burner, and incense and candles. Make the space your own, and place objects that help you connect with a sense of peace and tranquillity.

In summary, the following items are suggestions about what you may wish to put in your meditation space:
- You may have a table or shelf to put objects on.
- You may have a cupboard to place items in, which can be opened when your meditation practice takes place.
- A nice chair, cushions or a beanbag to sit on.
- Items to inspire: statues, pictures, etc.
- Nice covers and soft furnishings.
- A touch of nature, such as a plant or flowers.
- Crystals, special stones, feathers, etc.
- Aromas such as essential oils in a burner and incense.
- Candles.

Meditation Ideas to Get You Started

The following exercises are to get you started. They are here to help develop your practice and to help you explore ways of using meditation in a variety of settings (for ease of use they can also be found in the appendices).

Focusing on the Breath

The simplest form of meditation is to focus on the breath. This is also commonly known as mindful breathing.

Meditation does not have to be complicated. When we meditate, we should give permission to our conscious mind to be in a state of allowing and awareness. If thoughts arise, acknowledge them and let them go. If your mind wanders, gently bring your attention back to the breath.

First, find a quiet place where you will not be disturbed and sit comfortably. Close your eyes and take a nice, deep breath.

Bring your entire focus onto your breath. Take a nice breath in. As you breathe out, visualise all the stresses and strains of the day melting away. Breathe in and see that you are breathing in peace and relaxation. Breathe out all tension and worry.

Now focus on your feet for a moment. See them anchoring you to the earth, keeping you grounded. Now turn your attention back to the breath. Feel your chest gently rise up and down. Next, continue breathing normally as you relax. If your mind wanders, bring it back to the breath. Acknowledge any thoughts that may arise and see them float away as you continue to focus on the breath.

When you are done, bring your awareness back to your body. You may want to stretch. You may wish to focus on your feet grounding you into the earth. Be grateful for your experience and give thanks.

This simple meditation really can be done anywhere, once you get the hang of it. It can be done for a few moments on the bus or at work, sitting at your desk. Just take a few moments to focus on the breath and allow stresses and strains to slip away.

Standing Tall Meditation

This breath work can be done standing tall, like a mountain. Standing tall like a mountain is a common yet simple pose in yoga.

Stand with your feet in a comfortable position, hip distance apart. Focus on the soles of your feet connecting you to the earth, grounding you. Now visualise a cord running up your spine, coming out of the top of your head, pulling you up tall and straight. With your spine erect and your shoulders relaxed you are standing strong, like a mountain, with the cord connecting you to the heavens above and the ground below.

Now bring your attention to the breath. Allow all thoughts to float away. Take a few moments.

When you are ready, bring your awareness back to your body. You may wish to wriggle your toes or give your hands a slight shake to bring your awareness back.

This practice can literally be done while waiting in a queue, or at any time. No one needs to know you are doing it.

Walking Meditation

Similarly, the above can be done as part of a walking meditation. Instead of standing still, complete the exercise while moving. Just bring your focus to your feet and connect to the earth step by step, as you walk.

I like to do this when walking the dog out in nature. I focus on my feet connecting with the earth with each step, and with each step I visualise all tension leaving my body.

Focus Meditation

This is a good way to meditate if you struggle to focus on the breath, as instead you place your focus on an object. You can use a candle and its flame as a focus, or you can use an object such as an apple or a flower.

Sit comfortably, and take a few deep breaths as before. Visualise all tension leaving your body.

Now bring your awareness to the object. Gaze at it with a soft focus. Do not think of words to describe the object.

See the object without interpreting it. Now close your eyes for a while. If your mind wanders, gaze at the object again. You may even see the object in your mind's eye. Let go of all thoughts and relax. Complete your meditation practice when you are ready.

Eventually, with practice, you will begin to be able to meditate without the object there. Remember, meditation is an acquired skill that develops with practice and patience. Your concentration will improve gradually.

A commentator recently said that at an ashram they attended there were no fancy ways in which they were taught to meditate. They were told simply to breathe in, breathe out, sit, breathe in, breathe out, sit, breathe in, breathe out, sit. It was that simple.

The following is a slightly more involved process, which can be used as part of your daily practice once you've got used to the concept of meditation.

Meditation Exercise

Find a quiet place where you will not be disturbed. Unplug the phone. Switch the mobile off. Sit or lie comfortably. I prefer to sit, as this way I know I won't go to sleep. If you are sitting, make sure your feet are flat on the floor. If they are not, place a cushion or a book under your feet. Close your eyes and take a nice deep breath.

Focus on your feet. Visualise roots sprouting from your feet, anchoring you to the earth and grounding you. Draw up through these roots the energy of the earth, which will empower you and help to clear away all negative energy.

Now begin to focus on your breath. Take a deep breath in. When you breathe out, imagine all the stresses and strains of the day melting away. Breathe in and feel that you are breathing in peace and relaxation. Breathe out and see all the tension and worries melt away.

As you continue to breathe in, imagine that you are breathing in a pure white light. As you breathe out, imagine you are breathing out a grey mist. The grey mist is all the tension, worry, problems and niggles you may have encountered during the day.

Sit in this peace for five or ten minutes. If your mind wanders, bring it back to focus on your breathing. Focus on your chest, gently lifting it up and down as you breathe. Focus on the beat of your heart as it pumps the blood around your body. Acknowledge any thoughts that arise and see them float away into the ether.

When you are done, feel at peace and fully relaxed. If you can, try to do this for twenty minutes daily. But remember that even five minutes is better than no minutes.

At the end of your practice, surround yourself with a translucent bubble to help seal in the peace and to protect yourself from negative emotions. Be of joy and positivity and give thanks for the experience. See the bubble expand fifteen feet below you, fifteen feet above you and fifteen feet from each side of you, and fill it with love, light and peace.

Try to do this practice daily. You will be amazed at the benefit it will have on your health and well-being. There will be times when you do this practice that your mind keeps wandering. This is normal, so don't be put off. Perseverance is the key.

From this you can see that there are many ways of doing meditation. My husband likes to fish, and will spend many hours staring at a float. This, in a way, is a focus meditation. He feels the immense benefit of sitting for hours in the countryside staring at his float, and always comes home relaxed and at peace. Many people enjoy golf for a similar reason: the outdoors, the green of the grass, the trees, and concentrating on a small ball as it is knocked about the golf course. Running or jogging can also be considered a meditation (in fact, any exercise is good for getting rid of the toxins and negativity accumulated during the day).

Whenever you meditate, it's always good to visualise roots coming from the soles of your feet and grounding you to the earth, as in the previous meditation exercise. If you don't ground yourself during meditation you may feel out of touch with reality once your meditation practice is complete. If you feel spacey after a meditation practice, clap your hands and move or stamp your feet to shift the energy. It will help you become grounded.

There is a wealth of meditation and mindfulness circles that you can join. In the UK there are many Buddhist meditation groups that welcome new members. There are also many meditation groups run by individuals. Check online – or on social media, which is a good way to find groups. There are many apps available to download onto your phone or tablet, and also audio tracks. YouTube is also a valuable resource, among many other online resources.

Meditation Altar

Altars have been used in religious ceremonies for millennia. An altar is a place where you can connect with your divine self and feel a sense of spirituality and peace. It is a place to deeply connect with your meditation practice. It can be made to reflect your inner world: one of peace, serenity, harmony and balance. It should be a place where above all you find peace. Over time the atmosphere where your altar resides will change, so that when you enter your space you will immediately let go of any stresses and strains.

An altar in your home is a place to reflect, a refuge for you to enjoy and be peaceful in, and a place that gives you spiritual sustenance.

The altar can be set up on a shelf or on top of a chest of drawers. You can have more than one altar if you wish.

Place the altar where you can see it and where you can spend time in quiet reflection. Decorate your altar with a beautiful cloth. I like to choose a plain cloth in gold or white – something simple. Keep your altar clean and free from dust.

Decorate your altar space with pictures and statues, which will give inspiration and act as a portal to connect. You may wish to have a display of cut flowers on your altar to add life, scent and beauty. Be sure, though, to remove flowers that are dead and try not to let your altar get too cluttered.

Your altar can be made to appeal to the senses with things that are pleasing to the eye: fragrances, items that stimulate spirituality and peace, and sounds, for example meditation music or meditation instruments such as bells or singing bowls and the like.

Place a candle on your altar to light each time you spend time connecting and meditating. You can also use incense or aromatherapy oils in a burner to create beautiful aromas (make sure any candles or incense burn safely, and never leave flames unattended). You can use various coloured candles or just use a white candle. Candles symbolise spiritual light, bringing light to darkness, illumination, and revealing truths. Candles are good to use as part of a focus meditation. Light a candle and focus on the flame as all other thoughts or worries melt away.

Crystals, flowers, shells, bells and feathers make pretty additions to your altar, as well as pictures and photos. Make your altar as appealing as you can, as this is your space to connect.

Meditation Summary

Try to meditate daily. Try to find a time that is suitable for you, which you can stick to as part of a regular practice. You may prefer meditating in the morning, as I do, or in the evening when the kids are in bed. If you're new to meditation, start with just five minutes a day, increasing gradually to twenty minutes daily. The length of your meditation time can be built up over time. Don't try to force it. Let it develop naturally.

Make sure you sit in a comfortable position such as in a chair, and make sure your feet are connected to the floor. If you are short (like me), put a cushion or something similar under your feet. Sit with your back straight. If you're agile enough you can sit on the floor cross-legged like a yogi. You can lie down if you wish, but be careful not to fall asleep. Always remember to visualise the roots developing from your feet, grounding you.

At the end of your practice, record your experiences and how meditation makes you feel in a journal. This will help you reflect on how your meditation practice is developing and how it is affecting your overall sense of well-being.

Chapter Two

Connecting with Inner Awareness

All creativity comes out of inner spaciousness.
—Eckhart Tolle, 2009

In his book *A New Earth; Create a Better Life*, Eckhart Tolle states that practising what he calls 'conscious presence' can free us away from our world of thought and form, release us from the ego, and can also assist in achieving an inner stillness.

Presence is the place in which you become aware of the voice in your head and so achieve an awareness beyond thinking. The conscious presence is the state that resides in the now, the present moment, and not the past or the future. It's about finding the space between thinking and doing. This is called presence. It is achieved while focusing your attention on the act of doing and therefore putting mindfulness into action. It involves putting focused awareness into completing activities, which could be housework or washing the car, for example.

When you are aware of the voice in your head that continually tells stories and replays scenarios in the conscious mind, you begin to let go of these stories, and instead become a witness to them and accepting that they are there. This 'I Am' realisation attaches no judgement to thoughts. It is there as a witness and does not participate in thinking. As you connect with your presence behind your thoughts, the power of those thoughts loses its strength.

Eventually there exists a gap between thoughts, a space, within which there is an inner stillness: the letting go of the identification of me, the ego self. It consists of acknowledging that the thoughts are there but attaches no label to those thoughts.

Eckhart Tolle suggests that the egoic mind is conditioned by the past and by the identification of having things, items, and possessions. The identification with the ego creates attachment to things and a preoccupation of acquiring more things.

The ego also identifies with what Eckhart Tolle describes as the 'pain body'.

All things possess a specific vibrational frequency. Atoms, electrons and particles all come together to create physical objects that appear solid, such as a chair, a table or a door. Thoughts, Eckhart Tolle suggests, also resonate or vibrate at certain frequencies. Negative thoughts reside at the lower end of the spectrum, and positive thoughts reside at the higher end of the scale. The pain body identifies with the negative thoughts and so those negative thoughts feed the pain body (Eckhart Tolle, 2009).

The voice in your head will tell stories about other people, possibly painful, angry stories. These stories may be about the past, the future or even imaginary events, which can cause sadness, frustration or angst. The pain body will then feed off this drama.

Once you are aware of this concept, you may begin

to notice your own pain body, but also the pain body in others. Perhaps this could be someone who focuses solely on their illnesses and/or the illnesses of others, as if they feed off the attention this gives them.

In recognising that you have a pain body, you can begin to free yourself from it, as practising conscious presence can help you break out of the cycle of engaging in it. Through this realisation, the pain body can no longer control your thinking. It takes time and practice to break free from endless negative thinking, but persistence and the realisation of what is taking place can bring space between thoughts.

By aligning yourself into the present moment, the now, the grip of the ego will fall away. The stronger the ego, the more a person is separated from others. The present moment is ultimately all there ever is. The past has gone and cannot be revisited, and the future is not here yet.

Eckhart Tolle suggests asking the question,

'What is my relationship with the present moment?' In this way a state of presence can be brought about as you bring your awareness to it (Eckhart Tolle, 2009).

However, it is important, when thinking about the essence of time, that we do not confuse it with clock time, as we still need to be aware enough to make appointments, to get to work on time and to honour commitments or meet deadlines.

Practise this by bringing being into doing. This means being in the present while completing a task such as washing the dishes, dusting, gardening or other tasks. It is about the amount of presence you give to what you do and it is not about just completing tasks as a means to an end, a final goal. Try to establish a sense of acceptance and joy by being in alignment with the present moment.

Focused Awareness

One way to find space between thoughts is to bring awareness to the breath. Focused awareness of the breath can take your mind away from the repetitive stream of thought and thinking, and an inner stillness can be achieved. The more you practise bringing space between thoughts the easier it will get. When out walking, take time to look at a leaf, a flower. Appreciate its beauty.

Eckhart Tolle also suggests choosing an object, such as a cup or a plant. But the object must not be something that would stimulate the mind or a memory – for example, something that had writing on, which would provoke thinking. Give your complete attention to the object and let go of any thoughts about the object. Just observe the object and take the thinking out of perceiving.

Then, after a few minutes, take your gaze on to the surroundings. Listen to any sounds that may be around you, such as birds, the wind, the rain. With consistent practice this space between thoughts can be achieved and an inner stillness obtained.

Sometimes it may feel difficult to deal with certain people on a daily basis, especially in the world of work, where you may have no choice but interact with people who you may have conflict with or people who are too full of themselves and have large egos. If you take your focus to the present moment and don't dwell on other people's behaviours, dealing with those people will get easier over time. Bringing presence into your life is a gradual process, and the more you do it the easier it should become.

Learn to live in a different state of consciousness. Initially the ability to bring presence into moments may seem difficult in certain situations. By starting to develop presence it will become easier and easier to apply the principles, and if situations get difficult, remember that they will change.

Eckhart Tolle suggests using inner awareness as much as possible in everyday life. By taking a few conscious breaths during the course of the day, space or inner awareness can be brought into life. This is also referred to as space between thoughts. This inner space or awareness helps to break up the incessant chatter of the mind and can help bring about a sense of peace. Your breath, Eckhart Tolle suggests, is all you need to be aware of, even if you are a regular meditator.

This is excellent practice to do during the day, and a good habit to develop for bringing mindfulness into daily activities. Even if you have meditated in the morning or the previous evening, taking these mindful pauses helps to create an inner peace and an inner state of awareness, and keeps your awareness in the present moment and away from obsessive thoughts.

Developing Space Between Thoughts

We think millions of thoughts every day. Many of those thoughts are repetitive, and we allow those negative thoughts to permeate the mind. We live in a repeating narrative of what our thoughts dictate to us in a never-ending cycle. Many of those thoughts are core beliefs given to us in our childhood by our family, friends and peers, which give us our own limited beliefs. We identify, therefore, with our own thinking, and gain a sense of self from what is contained in our mind and in our thoughts. When we create the space between our thoughts we create an inner stillness, a peace within.

By developing space between thoughts through focusing on the breath, we create gaps within a constant stream of thoughts. Eckhart Tolle suggests this: one should not concern oneself with how long those gaps between thoughts should be; they can be short or even just for a few seconds. But by creating those gaps, that space, they will lengthen naturally. When consciousness is no longer taken over with thinking one can connect with inner peace (Eckhart Tolle, 2009).

Meditation and mindfulness, concentrating on the breath and being in the moment are examples of mindfulness practices. You just need to let go of stresses, concerns, worries, and just 'be'. If your mind wanders, bring it back to the breath.

There are many meditations and mindfulness exercises and activities that you can do, from sitting in silence and concentrating on the breath, to doing a more active walking meditation. These are explored in some of the chapters of this book. Don't get hung up, though, on not being mindful enough or having the thoughts in your head return. Just simply go back to being mindful once more.

By practising the path of non-resistance, by being non-judgemental and by practising non-attachment, you can become free and enlightened. Appreciate beauty and the simple things in life. Find contentment in your own company and the appreciation in life of others by practising love, kindness and compassion.

Mindfulness on the Go

Are you like me, and just don't seem to always have time to fit everything in? This raises the question: how can I fit in the practice of mindfulness when I'm always so busy?

Mindfulness is a very simple form of meditation, where you focus on the breath and are constantly aware of the moment. By being mindful, you focus only on the present moment, drawing your attention away from what is past or engaging in thinking about the future. The practice of mindfulness allows you to seize negative thinking before it tips you into a downward spiral. Practising mindfulness means looking at stressful situations as an observer and allowing those situations to pass by, rather like black clouds floating away over the horizon.

Meditation is a great tool in helping reverse the effects of stress and in calming the mind and emotions. When under threat, the adrenal glands release certain hormones so that the body can prepare for the fight or flight response. Once these hormones are released this in turn causes our muscles to tense and our blood pressure to increase, making our heart beat more intensely and making our breathing become faster and shallower.

Early on in my life I experienced quite severe panic attacks. This was in part my body's reaction to stress, and was part of my own fight or flight response. I regularly had panic attacks in big stores, thinking people were watching me. Through my practice of meditation and mindfulness, I no longer have regular panic attacks. When feelings or physical symptoms arise, I understand but also take time to observe them. I focus on what is happening, not why it is happening. In this way, I have the opportunity to be the observer. By bringing my attention to the breath I let the sensations float away and find calm in the situation.

So, how can we practise mindfulness on the go? Once you get the hang of it, it's quite easy to fit in little pockets of mindfulness during the day.

- Driving:
  Switch off the music, take a few deep breaths and focus on your breathing. Maintain full focus on the road, being mindful and present as you drive. If you feel your mind wandering off, bring it back to the road. Drive purposefully, don't rush, and don't react angrily to other drivers. Exercise kindness along your journey. Don't be an aggressive driver.

- Walking the dog (or any other walking activity):
  Focus on your feet and visualise all tension melting away into the earth as you walk. Bring your attention to the scenery: a tree, a flower, a leaf. Appreciate the beauty and the wonder around you. Be only in the present moment.

- Working:
  While sitting at your desk, take a few moments to connect with your breathing. Be present and at one with the moment. Take a few minutes before diving into any activity. Take a few moments to reconnect to the moment regularly during the day. If you have no desk, and you find yourself in a stressful situation, shut yourself in a toilet cubicle for a few minutes and take a few long, deep breaths. Allow yourself to focus on your breathing for a few moments and be present.

- At the gym:
  Here you really can focus on your breath. Be present and mindful of the moment. Be an observer. Allow your gym time to be part of your mindfulness, even if it is only for a few minutes.

- At various times in the day:
  Focus on the breath, find space and be present.

These are just a few ideas of mindfulness on the go. Being mindful is a skill that can be worked on at any time of the day. A few minutes here and there can add up during the day. The more you practise the easier it becomes. It's all about finding that inner space between moments that helps to calm the mind and ease the soul.

Chapter Three

Raising Your Spiritual Vibration

Everything in life is vibration.
—Albert Einstein

Everything in the universe is made up of energy and everything, including you, vibrates at a certain frequency. Atoms, continually vibrating, are the building blocks of everything, and everything is connected through various fields of energy. This energy constantly ebbs and flows like the tides of the sea.

As everything vibrates at a specific frequency, tables and doors, for example, appear solid, even though they are made up of atoms. These atoms vibrate at various speeds. Some vibrate at a faster speed, some at a slower speed. Humans have a vibrational field, not just in a physical form, but also in how their thoughts, feelings and emotions are at any given time.

As we evolve consciously we start to become more aware of how our mood and energy levels can be affected by what we take into our bodies and also how we are affected by our environments. The vibrational field that surrounds our bodies is known as the aura and is also known as the etheric field. As we develop our awareness, we begin to develop a sense of the auric field around our body and how our energy levels can be affected. Some people can see and sense the aura, even though scientists do argue that there is little evidence to support its existence.

Whether we believe in auras or not, there is no doubt that we need to be aware of how our body is affected by the substances we eat and drink. Everything that we eat and drink contains a life force energy and can affect our vibrational energy. Plus it's healthier to consume good food, so we should consider consuming foods that are of a high life force energy. Making changes to healthier, high-vibrational choices can help improve your emotional state, which in turn may help you deal with challenges in a more constructive manner and reduce the impact of negative emotions such as anger.

As you develop more spiritually and mindfully you may notice that inappropriate eating habits fall away naturally. You may find yourself becoming more sensitive to certain things and give up on addictive substances and behaviours.

Vibrational Fields

Even if you are not aware of fields of vibration, you will know what I mean when I say that you can detect certain vibes or energies in a room, atmospheres in buildings or the energies emanated by a person due to their mood or emotions. For example, the peaceful atmosphere of a church or the uncomfortable feeling you get upon entering a room after an argument.

Some people are more sensitive to vibrational fields or energies that others. The ones who are sensitive to the moods and energies of people and places tend to be empaths, people who tend to take on board the world's stresses and joys. Many people on the spiritual, mindful path tend to be empathic and sensitive, and absorb emotions like a sponge.

As we go about our daily business, we encounter many different energy fields that can have an impact on our own personal energy fields. We may also come across varying energies and individuals, different moods and emotions throughout the day.

During the course of the day we also interact with various energetic fields, which emanate from mobile phones, computers, artificial lighting and other mechanical devices. Any appliance that is connected to an electricity supply will emit electrical and magnetic fields when switched on. These electrical fields may be invisible, but they can have an effect on our own energetic fields.

The energetic vibration of nature with its natural colours, lights and sounds, for example, is very different to that of an artificial environment such as an office, with its artificial lighting, electrical equipment and harsh furniture.

We interact daily with different people, different temperaments and different personalities. Sometimes we may enter into conflict with these individuals. They may take their temper out on us, or they may be anxious or stressed. The emotions that emanate from individuals will undoubtedly have an effect on our own energy vibration. Have you ever started the day in a good mood, only to come across someone who leaves you feeling drained and depleted? My very close friend calls these people 'mood hoovers', and I quite like that analogy.

In his book *A New Earth*, Eckhart Tolle states, 'Every human being emanates an energy field that corresponds to his or her inner state, and most people can sense it, although they may feel someone else's energy emanation only subliminally. That is to say, they don't know that they sense it, yet it determines to a large extent how they feel about and react to that person.' (Eckhart Tolle, 2008).

This paragraph succinctly puts into words how we may feel at the moment when we meet people for the first time. Some we instantly like, others we take a sudden dislike to. This indicates how we may be tuning into the other person's vibrational field on an unconscious level.

When you vibrate at a higher vibrational level, you feel happier, healthier and lighter. When you vibrate at a lower level you will feel heavier, unhealthy, anxious and unsettled. There are many ways of helping to elevate your vibrational field and energies, and one way can be through the role of mindfulness, meditation, exercise and diet.

Diet

A good diet, as we know, is beneficial for our health and well-being, as well as playing an important role in keeping our energies high. By being mindful of what we take into our bodies and eating high-vibrational foods we can assist in keeping our energies elevated, can help with stress and can improve the overall quality of our lives.

Everything that we eat and drink has a life force energy. Fresh vegetables, organic produce, wholefoods, nuts, fruits, fresh herbs and fresh produce have a higher life force energy than other foods. A suitable water intake is also paramount. If you eat meat, choose organic where possible, from animals reared ethically. Foods that are alive, such as plant-based foods and fresh fruit and vegetables, have a higher life force energy than processed, chemically enhanced foods, sodas and alcohol. Even cutting back a little on processed, unhealthy foods can have a positive effect on your energy levels, mood, well-being and overall health. Eating less meat is not only kinder to your body, but current thinking is that it is also better for the environment and reduces the suffering of animals.

Cutting back on foods and substances that are bad for you, such as alcohol, caffeine, tobacco, and drugs, can all assist in improving your overall health and raising your vibrational levels. Other foods that affect your vibrational fields, which can be eaten in more moderation, are processed foods, products made with white flour, foods with a high sugar content, sodas and dairy products. A plant-based diet with organically grown produce, where possible, and drinking more water, will assist in improving your health and well-being. Even the smallest of changes can be beneficial in raising your vibrational energies and will assist in improving your health and well-being.

To lift the vibration of the food you are eating you may want to take time to give thanks, especially if you eat meat or poultry, which has given its life for the purpose of consumption. It's also a way to be mindful about what you eat. And try to take time to chew your food slowly.

There are many ways of improving the way you eat. Be guided by what works for you and what makes you happy, because happiness in itself raises your vibration.

Exercise

Exercise is not only beneficial to your health and well-being but can also elevate your energies and your mood. Any type of aerobic exercise that has you breathing more rapidly will increase your energy flow. Yoga, tai chi and qigong are gentle forms of exercise that traditionally focus the movement of chi or the life force energy. Martial arts are also excellent for this but require more discipline and a certain level of fitness. Walking in nature, connecting with the earth and the high-vibrational frequencies contained in plants and trees, is wonderful for elevating your energies and enhancing your mood. Any exercise can alleviate stress, promote your health and well-being, generally get you fit and help you feel better (start at your own pace and consult a doctor or healthcare professional if you have any health concerns before undertaking any strenuous forms of exercise).

Other Ways to Raise Your Energies

There are many ways to raise your vibration, improve your mood, uplift your emotions and give a general improvement to your sense of well-being. These include meditation, gratitude, watching less television and violent media productions, right action, positive thinking, forgiveness and love. All these topics are covered in other chapters, but are also summarised here.

Our vibrational frequency emanates from our thoughts, emotions and actions throughout the day. Our alignment to the energies around us (and our own personal vibrational frequencies) dictates what we attract. Therefore, a higher vibrational state that is more positive in nature will attract more positive and uplifting experiences and people. This is known as the universal law of attraction: what you give out you get back. You can create change according to how you regulate your thoughts and emotions.

By becoming conscious of your thoughts you have the ability to raise your vibration by activating thoughts that are in harmony with your well-being and the well-being of others. Instead of thinking negative thoughts about yourself or others, being judgemental, angry, jealous or having feelings of guilt, change them to thoughts of forgiveness, gratitude, love, compassion and kindness. Give without expecting anything in return. Try to do a good deed each day for others, even if it's something as simple as letting someone out in traffic.

Make it a regular part of your day to sit in quiet contemplation. Meditation helps alleviate stress and can set you up for the day or get you ready for a peaceful night's sleep. It helps calm the body and the mind.

Make your home and surroundings a vibrational match to your desire of elevated energy levels. Declutter your home, give your space a lick of paint and take time to declutter where you can. Place objects that give pleasure and raise the vibration of your space in your home. Include plants and crystals and inspiring statues, such as Buddhas or angels, and uplifting pictures.

Reduce your exposure to television programmes that are not uplifting or are violent in nature. Limit your time watching the news, as many news stories are designed to invoke fear and contain very little in the way of uplifting or inspiring accounts, as they focus on war, famine and violent acts.

Fear sells. That's how the media make their money. The news and the media try to get us hooked on fear: advertising revenue is greater during the news broadcasts, as the news gets us hooked and engaged in fearful stories from around the world.

Obsessively focusing on the doom and gloom of the world portrayed in the mainstream media is not healthy.

Many stories are sensationalised for the biggest impact. Sensationalist headlines sell newspapers, and gossip columns sell magazines. Many headlines online are sensationalist to get more clicks. Don't convince yourself that you are a bad person for not focusing on every traumatic event or suffering in the world. You can't take on responsibility for everyone else's pain or misery, and to focus solely on such things isn't healthy. Instead, try to focus on the good in the world rather than the bad. Shift your focus to something more positive and step away from drama.

Choose to be in the company of people who support, inspire and uplift you. As you choose to surround yourself with people who elevate your mood, you will naturally tune into their higher vibrations.

Using Visualisation to Strengthen and Protect the Auric Field

As we develop spiritually with mindfulness and meditation, we may find that we become more and more sensitive to the energies that surround us, both environmentally and through other people. We encounter many energy fields during the day, including electrical fields that surround items such as computers and mobile phones, and these can affect and interact with our own energy field. We may come across people who are emotionally demanding or draining and people who are generally negative or angry, or we may work in stressful environments that are harmful to our emotional and physical well-being. Unfortunately, many of these things can't be avoided. Even our own thought patterns or behaviour can be negative. Protecting and strengthening our auric field becomes essential as we encounter these various energies during our day.

Ways to Find Calm

Meditation is a good way to strengthen our energy field, as it gives us calmness by quietening the mind, calming the bodily processes and alleviating stress and anxiety (see the chapter on meditation).

Another good way is to have a soak in the bath. Adding a handful of Epsom salts (magnesium sulphate crystals) to your bathwater is a good way to cleanse the auric field, or you can sprinkle a handful of unrefined natural sea salt or rock salt into your bath. Epsom salts are cheap to buy. When put in a bath they help in the removal of toxins and can help to relax the body and mind.

Make your bath time a calming experience and let go of anything not of peace. You may wish to light candles or use pure essential oils to add aromas. A few drops of essential oil added to your bathwater can also have healing and relaxation qualities. Soak for around twenty minutes, or longer if you wish. Visualise the water cleansing your aura and taking away all that negative spiritual debris you have picked up during the day, in addition to cleansing you physically. After your bath ensure that you rest fully and drink plenty of water. If you don't have a bath, or don't like taking a bath, visualise the water from a shower cleansing away all the negativity. In addition, if you are a reiki practitioner you can use your symbols as well.

Using these techniques can help keep the negative debris we encounter daily under control. The more positive we feel about ourselves, the more positive experiences we can attract in our daily life.

Smudging

Smudging is an ancient, traditional ritual practice of burning bundles of herbs to cleanse and purify the environment, homes, items or people to rid them of negative energies, leaving only positive ones. Traditionally sage is used. Bundles of sage can be bought from any New Age store or online. By burning bundles of sage, the user visualises any negative dense, vibrational energies being cleared away, leaving the energy cleansed and positive. It's a great way to uplift the energies in a home, especially where there has been aggression, violence or disputes in the home. Even watching violent movies or playing violent video games can leave dense energies, which may be stuck.

Crystals and other items can also be cleansed by using a smudge stick. Often people are cleansed by smudging ahead of any ritual. In the Catholic Church, incense is still used as a way of purification.

Regular smudging can help raise the vibrational energy of the particular environment in which you use it. You know yourself if you enter a room after an argument you can probably feel the dense energy there, and it may make you feel uncomfortable.

Begin by setting the intention to cleanse the home of negative energy by the act of smudging. Objects such as crystals can also be cleansed this way by passing the item through the smoke and visualising the negative energy being removed. You can also cleanse people by passing the smoke around the auric field.

To do this, light the end of the smudge stick and blow out the flame. Put the smudge stick on a plate or on an abalone shell to catch any burning embers. Waft the smoke, using either your hand or a feather fan. You may have to blow on the smudge stick regularly to encourage more smoke. As you go around the home, visualise the smoke from the smudge stick removing all negative vibrations and stuck energy, leaving only positive energies.

The Path of Least Resistance and Raising Vibrations

The term 'path of least resistance' specifically refers to living in the now.

The shape and quality of your thoughts, Wayne Dyer explains, can put up resistant thoughts. Aligning your thoughts to what is creative, positive, tranquil and peaceful, while also letting go of stress, helps raise your vibrational energy in a positive way. Once your vibrations are raised, this then allows your creative processes to formulate themselves. In making positive lifestyle choices to raise our vibrational energies we can ultimately develop a better connection with the universe and attract what we want in life.

'Path of least resistance' is a term used in many spiritual texts. It is about going with the flow of life and about putting up the least resistance to the circumstances in your life. This doesn't mean that you shouldn't put effort into work or achieving goals, but that you should take perfect action at the right time. It's a balancing act of striving to achieve. But, if barriers come up that seem insurmountable, it's about letting go, and not putting up a fight against circumstances that go against you.

Everything in life is there for a purpose, even the barriers. They may be there to push you in another direction or to guide you in some another way that you possibly never considered. By remaining in the present moment, but yet focused, other ways may be illuminated to take you on your path. Be in the present moment and in a constant state of allowing rather than putting up resistance. This term is referred to in one of my favourite books by Wayne Dyer, *The Power of Intention* (2010).

When you love yourself and respect yourself, you bring yourself into alignment with the field of intention, the one that the universe intends for you. This doesn't mean loving yourself in an egotistical way. It means loving yourself for who you truly are and with the complete acceptance of who you are without self-criticism. You live in a universe that is unlimited. The only person who limits you is you. As long as the ego is present you will offer some resistance, by way of resistant thoughts. So change your thoughts to those where resistance is minimised. Thoughts that create bad feelings are those resistant thoughts. These bad thoughts put up a barrier between you and what you want to attract into your life.

By applying thoughts of minimal resistance into your daily mindset, you will train yourself to make this your natural way of reacting to the world and those around you. In this way you will eventually become the peaceful, stress-free person you want to be. You will then in turn attract peaceful, stress-free experiences into your existence. For example, I try no longer to react to people in an angry, aggressive or argumentative manner. By choosing not to react, my life has developed into one that is more peaceful, calm and relatively stress-free.

To flow in the path of least resistance, it is vital to shape your thoughts so that they are in alignment with the universe. Poor thoughts are resistant thoughts. An example of having resistant thoughts would be to have negative, stressful thoughts instead of positive thoughts. If you wish to live a stress-free and tranquil life it is essential to retrain your thoughts to those that are in alignment with how you want to feel. When stressful and negative thoughts arise, train your mind to let go of those negative thought patterns and replace them with more positive thoughts. Make it a daily habit to harmonise your thoughts and to not dip down into negative, fear-based thinking.

If you wish to find happiness, be that happiness. If you wish to find love, be that love. Align your thoughts to those of happiness and love. Be in a constant state of allowing rather than resisting, and allow loving, peaceful, happy thoughts to flow throughout your day.

We live in an abundant universe, in a time when we can create whatever we choose. We have the world at our fingertips and knowledge that can be accessed in an instant, yet many of us live in despair, experience negative thought processes, and put up resistance to allowing all that is good into our lives.

Writing and Using Positive Affirmations

Writing and using positive affirmations can also help raise our vibrations. The use of positive affirmations can allow creative energy to develop while aligning those creative processes to the universe. The use of positive affirmations can also help change thought patterns, bring them into the field of conscious intention, and align them with the universe.

An affirmation is a verbal description of the desired condition that you wish to achieve, and can be used to create the reality that we require. Affirmations should be positive and in the present tense and preferably short, so that they can be remembered. By repeating an affirmation and knowing what you are saying and why you are saying it, your mind will come into a state of consciousness where it will accept what you are repeating as true.

Positive affirmations are phrases that you consistently repeat to yourself. They can contain within them either a specific outcome or what you wish to develop. With constant repetition the affirmations will start to be accepted by your subconscious mind, even if these statements may not be initially true.

By feeling bad you can create an anxious state, which then can cause resistance to allowing any positive changes to manifest. You can align to the divine creative state, the state of allowing and being, by aligning yourself to positive thoughts and feelings. By permitting yourself to realise your full potential as a human being you can become a beacon of hope for others, a shining light and an inspiration.

Make the choice to feel good about yourself and others and the world around you.

Ultimately, we are the result of what we think and feel about ourselves and the world around us. Any positive intentions we have can be weakened by low energy thoughts, and this can impose restrictions on what we wish to attract in life.

Thoughts of fear, shame, guilt, anger, stress and other lower vibrational thoughts can result in us manifesting further lower vibrational energies. This in turn may result in us taking out our resentments on others by developing unkind and uncaring attitudes. We could even end up hurting those who we love and who mean the most to us.

What we give out we receive: like attracts like. When you

are kind you receive kindness back. When you react from a place of anger and pain these energies will ultimately be reflected back to you.

When you align your being with positive intent the universe will send opportunities that are in keeping with your soul's purpose, and when you align your thoughts in conjunction with your divine nature you will be in harmony and balance.

You will increase your ability to manifest great things when you align yourself to your true nature. This is your divine purpose. This is the true essence of your being, and it's vital to not work against it. Non-harmonious energy comes from non-harmonious thoughts and feelings. When we are harmonious our energy level will naturally be elevated, and our spiritual vibrations will be lifted.

As Wayne Dyer says in his book, 'As you practise being in a state of allowing and living a life of least resistance, success is what you become, not what you choose. It becomes what you are, your natural state of being. Abundance will no longer evade you, it will flow to you unimpeded.' (Wayne Dyer, 2010).

Know and feel abundance as part of your natural state of being.

Chapter Four

Kakeibo – The Art of Money Mindfulness

Kakeibo, pronounced 'kah-keh-boh', is the Japanese art of saving, a way of mindfulness with money. The word kakeibo translates to 'household financial ledger'. It was founded by Japan's first female journalist, a lady by the name of Hani Motoko, in 1904.

The art of kakeibo can help streamline expenses, set saving goals, apply mindfulness to spending habits and help gain control over household finances.

Kakeibo has a journaling approach, which helps you to manage your incomings and outgoings effectively. It also helps you evaluate any unnecessary expenses that you can eliminate, so that money can be then saved or invested. Many people, for example, set up direct debits and then forget about them, therefore wasting money each month.

Let's face it. For most of us saving is difficult at the best of times. I started to use kakeibo myself when I realised just how much unnecessary debt I'd accumulated over the years. At this point the realisation struck that I had to act instead of sticking my head in the sand and hoping that somehow my debts would just miraculously disappear.

Being consumed with the daily activities of life, I just

hadn't realised how much debt I'd racked up. I had an overdraft that was never reduced and constantly in use, credit card debts that were always paid monthly but at the minimum amount, and online catalogue debts that could be doubled at the click of a mouse without my realising just how much I'd spent.

Shockingly, I found out that by just paying the minimum payment each month, for the average person with the national average credit card debt, it would take them around twenty-five years to pay it off in full.

This just shows how problematic credit card debt could become. I, like many, had stuck my head in the sand, believing that by paying the minimum each month I was somehow making a more significant impact on the debt than I actually was, whereas in reality I needed to pay much more each month.

This scenario will resonate with many people. Applying the principles of kakeibo to money can help take away a lot of stress and worry, and this in turn can assist in helping to take control of your life and ultimately spending habits that have spiralled out of control. Stressing about finances at the end of the day doesn't contribute to a mindful state, and can ultimately put a strain on close relationships.

Kakeibo helps you keep financially mindful. By recording your daily spending in a journal you will have greater control of your incomings and outgoings. Writing every transaction in a journal helps you reflect on your spending and consider impulse purchases. Part of the kakeibo method is to ask, 'Is it necessary?' You then take time to pause and consider whether the purchase is a need or a want. Do you actually need that item, or do you just want it? If you take time to think about and reflect on a purchase you can work out if it really is needed. If the purchase really is needed then the purchase can be made.

The key to kakeibo is to write everything down. There are specifically printed kakeibo journals available to help you do this.

Kakeibo Journal

A typical journal will have space for you to record your income and outgoings for the month, space to write your goals for the month, and room to detail how you will achieve them.

Expenses are divided into four main categories. These are survival, optional, cultural and extra.

The survival category includes expenses such as food, medicines, travelling, and so on.

The optional category covers such expenses as pub outings, restaurants, takeaways, etc.

The cultural category contains items such as books, magazines, shows, music, and so on.

The extra section is for recording things such as repairs, unexpected expenses, gifts, and the like.

At the end of the month you will review your spending according to each category to see if you achieved the goal you set yourself at the beginning. Then you write a short reflection on how your spending has developed and how you intend to improve your spending in the following month.

As you can see, it's not just about recording expenses. It's also about goal setting and reflecting on your spending habits to see if there are patterns to your spending and evaluating if those patterns can be altered in any way. By reviewing your spending activity you can identify any areas where cuts may be made to save towards future goals.

Recording income and expenditure is at the centre of kakeibo.

When starting, ask yourself the following questions:

1. How much money is coming in?
2. How much do I want to save?
3. How much do I spend?
4. How can I improve?

As already mentioned, a ready-made journal can be used for this activity (there are many available in stores and online). Or you can use a blank journal to make your own, using the four categories above. The journal, in whatever form, can be carried with you, ready to record items.

Like any journaling activity, it is best to get into a good habit of incorporating it into your daily routine. Consistency is key. The journal will be specifically for recording finances and will be used for no other purpose. Physically writing things down changes behaviours, in the same way that food journaling changes eating habits. Think of it as a money diet.

Thinking about purchases for twenty-four hours before buying can also help align your spending habits. Taking the time to think about purchases will go in some way to indicate whether you really want or actually need the item, as many purchases are made on impulse. Question yourself continually. For example, that item of clothing you are looking at … do you really need it? Or is it purely a want?

Kakeibo is a great way to organise your spending. It helps you plan your finances, makes you think carefully about spending, and assists you in achieving those financial goals. Using the kakeibo budgeting method will help you to get into the habit of recording your expenditure on a daily basis.

By thinking about your spending you could possibly save as much as 35 per cent of your expenditure, compared to what you spend now. Try to think of areas where you could cut costs. For example, consider taking a packed lunch to work rather than spending money in the canteen. Instead of buying that expensive coffee on the way to work, take a flask of coffee instead. Instead of spending money on a takeaway, consider eating at home, and perhaps make a 'fakeaway'. Look at your shopping habits. Do you have an online account with a supermarket and do you just buy the same items each week? Can you buy the supermarket's own brands rather than high-end brands? Can you shop at other, cheaper, lower-end supermarkets that don't sell branded products? If you analyse your spending you will find that there are many ways to cut costs.

At the end of each month, re-examine your spending habits. Have you achieved your spending goals? Try to see if there are any areas that may require readjusting.

By achieving those saving goals you really can work your way to the life you desire.

Chapter Five

The Abundance Mindset

What does abundance mean to you? Material success? Or does it mean the freedom of choice, or possibly the flow of opportunities? Perhaps it means that you have enough of everything, whether that be food, nice clothes, money, happiness or a fantastic family life.

Abundance can mean many things to different people.

Stephen R. Covey, in his book *The 7 Habits of Highly Effective People*, coined the term 'abundance mentality'. The abundance mentality, he stated, comes out of a profound inner sense of security and personal worth (Covey, 2004). In other words, abundance is all about how you think. Wayne Dyer stated that abundance is not something you acquire, but it is something that you tune into.

So, ultimately, abundance is a state of mind. We can put up resistance to abundance when we enter into a negative statement about what we do or don't have and engage in negative self-talk, convincing ourselves about what we lack. These statements are very easily said to our inner self. They tell us that we don't have enough or that there is a lack of something. Or they even create envy of things that

our neighbours may have that we don't. We've all been there, making statements such as:
- I haven't got enough.
- I don't have enough money to…
- There's not enough to go around.
- I don't know how I'm going to pay for…

Covey called this the 'scarcity mentality'.

Abundance comes in many forms. It is not just to do with money. An abundance of opportunities, time, energy, love, fulfilling relationships, joy, happiness, and meaningful experiences can all be expressed abundantly.

By being in a natural state of allowing and keeping our inner dialogue positive we can truly attract all the abundance we ever need.

The universe is in a constant state of supplying, but it is up to us to align our thoughts in such a way that we tap into this universal supply and are ready and open to receive it. We need to take steps to visualise and allow the abundance to flow into our lives. Allowing any thought of scarcity or shortage impedes the flow of abundance and allows it to be replaced by a state of want.

Success means different things to different people. Success isn't just the acquisition of material things. It's a mindset, something you tune into. This is how the law of attraction works. By allowing your state of mind to tune into the abundant universe you get what you put out there. In other words, what you give out to the universe you get back.

Wayne Dyer advocated the practice of allowing and establishing a path of least resistance. By doing this you allow abundance to flow through you and flow to you, unimpeded by resistant thoughts.

You should be careful, Dyer suggested, not to hoard or to cling tightly to material things that manifest in your life. Life must be free-flowing, not stagnant. This is the nature of energy: staying in a constant free-flowing state of allowing and non-resistance, like water flows constantly in a river. Be like water, and flow.

Be in a state of constant giving and receiving. Give things away that you no longer use. Recycle them, give them to charity and declutter your home. By doing so you free up the space and energy to receive more.

Abundance Mindset Summary

These are ten steps to abundance, taken from Wayne Dyer's book *The Power of Intention* (2010). I have summarised them here:

1. See the world as an abundant place, full of possibilities, and above all as a friendly, not hostile, place.
2. Affirm to yourself that you attract abundance and success because that is who you are.
3. Stay in a state of allowing. Do not put up resistance, and remain in a state of harmony. Get rid of any thoughts of doubt or negativity.
4. Make a choice to stay in the present moment, in the now. When you dwell on the past or think too much about the future, you may put up resistant or negative thoughts. Focus on this current moment and the now.
5. Act on feelings of abundance. Act as if abundance is already here. This does not mean that you should spend money recklessly. This is about having an abundance mindset. Act with passion and with confidence.

6. Remember that the more abundance and prosperity come your way the more you will be able help others. The more you have, the more you will have to share with those around you.
7. Continually feel inspired. When you are inspired, you are in tune with the universe. Feel the high energy of positive emotions. Don't dip into low-level energy emotions of anger, despair, anxiety, and so on.
8. Don't impede the flow of energy by hoarding or clinging on to what you receive. Practise detachment from material things.
9. Meditate to tune into the universe as the source of your abundance and success.
10. Cultivate an attitude of gratitude. Be thankful for what you have and what you will receive. Look upon the worst times of your life with gratitude, for they make you the person you are today.

(Adapted from Wayne Dyer, 2010.)

We live in an abundant universe, and we all have within us the ability to experience a happy and abundant life. You possess within you the ability to transcend the illusion of life and to create a better reality for yourself and others, one greater than you could ever have thought possible. You have within you the ability to change your destiny for the better. The only thing that stops you is you.

Chapter Six

Finding Your Life's Purpose

In his research, Dr Abraham Maslow found that those who feel purposeful live their lives to the highest fulfilment and achieve self-realisation, and in doing so they become everything that a person can become. This state is defined as achieving contentment with yourself through the activation of your full potential of talents and abilities.

The psychological self-realisation to me is the equivalent to God-realisation in the spiritual sense. They are one and the same, but not everyone believes in God.

Ultimately in life, whether on the spiritual path or simply trying to find your way in life by whatever method, self-realisation is or should be the goal to which you aspire. Self-realisation, by definition, is the fulfilment of your own potential.

It is the quest of many to seek and discover their life's purpose, a purpose that evades many. It certainly evaded me for many years.

Most self-realised people know their life's purpose, and when they do you will notice that they eat, live, sleep and breathe it. It's their passion.

So why is a chapter on finding your life's purpose in a

book of everyday practices? It is because finding your life's purpose is an intention that you can connect to daily. It is how you carry out your daily life and duties. It is the essence of who you are and who you aspire to be.

A State of Allowing

It is not all about constantly *seeking* to connect to your soul's purpose. It is more about putting your mind into a state of *allowing* your soul's purpose to manifest.

A state of allowing is how your daily practice should begin. You should start your day, each day, by putting trust into the universe, and when you are in this constant state of allowing, it will reveal to you your life's purpose.

There are no accidents. You are here on purpose. When you are in a state of allowing, it is not so much about what you feel but how you feel. It is action in inaction. It is not so much in your physical activities but in your mindset. Believe that your purpose in life will reveal itself to you. Connect with your soul. It knows what to do.

When you align to your soul's purpose your life will become more harmonious, and synchronicities in life will begin to appear. Opportunities, people and events may appear that will put you on the path of self-realisation (the fulfilment of your own potential).

Now take time to ask yourself these questions. What inspires you? What does your inner knowing say to you?

Know and feel the universe coming together, assisting you in aligning to your soul's purpose. Allow the universal law of attraction to align with your being and know that the universe is co-creating to allow people and opportunities into your life that will assist you in manifesting your divine life's purpose. See, in your mind's eye, the divine plan unfold and allow it to do so. Do not force anything. Just be in a constant state of allowing.

Allowing Changes

Changes may begin to happen. They may or may not be sudden. They may be subtle changes that ease you on your life's journey. Or they may be part of your divine plan, or be connected to your journey to self-realisation. You may be compelled to give up addictive substances or obsessive behaviours, or make healthier lifestyle or relationship choices. You might begin to seek out more like-minded people, take up new activities that expand the mind, or new training regimes to gain a healthier body. You may become a healer, a teacher, a therapist. Or you many inspire others and meditate more. You may sense things that once gave you great pleasure seem empty and meaningless, such as watching hours of television, playing video games or whiling your hours away in a pub or bar. You may be inspired to live your life in a more meaningful way.

To do all these things and make the changes to lead a more meaningful life, a life on purpose, you will need to take action steps. However, if blocks to your progress arise don't force things. Know that any blocks to your progress are there for a reason. Take time to tune into your intuition and go with what feels right. Also, remain detached to the opinion of others, however well-meaning they may be. Sometimes what we truly want or desire is not in keeping with our life's purpose or with people's visions of what they think that we should be doing. This is your life to live and your path, not theirs. They are not you.

Live the life that you are destined to live. Listen to those internal callings. Take time to listen to that inner voice. We are here to fulfil an inner purpose and we are part of an infinite intelligence that knows why we are here. We just need to tune into that inner knowing.

When I was thirty, I found myself with two small children. My youngest was a baby. We as a family were virtually bankrupt. Why did I find myself on the verge of bankruptcy? I had invested in a business that gave me no joy, which I could not afford to run. It was a millstone around my neck. I had invested in that business in effect to please others. It left me depressed and floundering in a big, black hole, financially and emotionally. I felt that I had no way out, and it even led me to thoughts of suicide.

I woke up one morning and pleaded with the universe to give me answers. It was just not meant to be like this. This was not what I signed up for, not what I was on the earth to do. I read a lot of self-help books at the time and asserted to myself that the universe was going to conspire to help me. I changed my mindset.

Bankruptcy was imminent but I asserted to myself that I could find a way to get out of it. All was not lost. Nothing was impossible. I put the shop up for sale. Someone offered me a sum of money, less than what it was worth, for everything in the shop. It was not a lot but it meant that I had cash in my pocket and everything would be cleared away for me. So I took it.

There were still two years left on the lease for the shop. I asserted to myself that somehow we would be able to pay for it. Miraculously, the owners of the shop cancelled the lease, unexpectedly freeing us from the debt. I later found out that the shop was to be taken over by a large betting firm.

Both my husband and I found jobs that we continued in for many years and which gave us job satisfaction. Our debts were paid in full within five years. We never went to court, never went bankrupt. I was absolutely focused on paying off all our debts, and we did. I put my faith in the universe, and as if by magic it paid us back in full and changed our lives for the better.

At this time I also qualified as a complementary therapist and have followed the spiritual path ever since, meditating and doing my best to live in a more positive way. Although life still presents its ups and downs, I cope much better and know that any challenges that arise are there for a reason. I know in my heart of hearts that the universe is on my side, and I put my trust in it to provide for me and my family.

Through my therapies and my constant learning, I came to write my books. This I know is my ultimate life purpose, which has been revealed to me after waiting for a long time: to share my knowledge with others.

By consciously aligning yourself to a place of trust and faith, the universe will guide you to your life's purpose. Remember that you are a part of a divine universal consciousness, and as such you have before you a divine plan for life. You were set upon this earth to follow a purpose, and the universe will conspire to align your path to that same purpose. The trick is to let go of the fight, the resistance, the questioning and to allow that universe in its wondrous form to show you your true path in life and your potential. When you serve others, your life's path will unfold. You don't seek. You allow. When you align to your life's purpose your life will become more harmonious. Synchronicities will begin to appear. Opportunities, people and events will begin to materialise that will help put you onto the path of self-realisation (the fulfilment of your own potential).

These changes might not be sudden. They may be subtle changes, easing you along your life's journey. You may be compelled to make life changes: give up addictive substances, become vegetarian, practise yoga, start to make healthier life choices. You might seek out like-minded people, learn new skills, become a healer, teach others, meditate more. You may sense things that once gave you pleasure, such as spending endless time in the pub or bar, or watching endless hours of television, seem empty and fall away. You may find yourself wanting to live your life in a more constructive and meaningful way.

Your soul's (or higher self's) divine mission is to guide you to your life purpose, the reason why you were set on this earth. Accessing the soul part of you, your higher self, can set you on a course to self-realisation, to a greater connection to the divine source, to the universal consciousness you call God. You might notice these synchronicities and events unfolding as they serve some divine plan.

When you know that you are here, ready for a purpose, you should align your thoughts and ideas so that they are in balance with what you wish to set out to do. Allow the universal law of attraction to align with your being and know that the universe is co-creating to allow people and opportunities that will assist you in manifesting your divine purpose in life. See this divine plan unfold and allow it to do so. Be in a state of allowing. Do not force it, but at the same time be sure to take action steps towards your goal. Don't force things if resistance or obstacles occur. Those obstacles might be there for a reason. Take time to check in with your own intuition. Take some time in a quiet space to check in with your inner guidance, and ask yourself what feels right and what doesn't. Visualise scenarios. Do they inspire you and feel good, or do they feel uninspiring and difficult? Take time to tune into what feels right.

Know and feel the universe coming together, aligning with your soul's purpose – the reason why you are here on this earth – and allow the divine plan put before you to unfold. When you are aligned with your life's purpose you will feel joy and enthusiasm in following your path. Actively feel the universe cooperating to offer you the wondrous opportunities needed so that you can fulfil your mission in life.

Finding my life's purpose was something that evaded me for years. I had a rough idea of what my life's purpose was, but it was something that just didn't seem to manifest for me. When I listened to spiritual call-in shows online, or read spiritual books, the most frequently asked question seemed to be, 'How do I find my life's purpose?'

It came to a point when I realised that I had to stop searching for the answers and asking the same old questions, like, 'Should I do this? Should I do that?' Instead I had to take a step back and somehow put myself into a place of faith and trust in the universe, with the knowledge that I was exactly where I was meant to be, doing exactly what I was meant to do. I felt that life would unfold exactly as it should, while simultaneously and consciously I knew that I needed to consciously align myself to my life's purpose and that it would reveal itself in due course.

Prior to this I had spent many years chasing what I thought I should be doing, and it had always ended in disaster. I would constantly chase a vision of what I thought my life would be, rather than allowing things to happen. When I forced things, even though I knew deep down they weren't right for me, it would turn into a calamity. Because I am a people-pleaser, I tried to please my family by doing what they thought I should do, and this was ultimately wrong.

Things began to take shape when I took a step back and allowed the universe to work its power. Things began to manifest with more ease once I aligned myself into a conscious state of allowing. This did not mean that I was lazy and didn't look for opportunities coming my way. Rather, I began to allow events to reveal themselves rather than trying to force things. If something wasn't meant to be or circumstances were stacking up against me, I would take a step back and let things unfold in time. I also had to learn patience. Whenever I do anything now I ask myself, 'Does it align me to my purpose?', 'Does it give me joy?', 'Does it take me away from the Creator/God or does it bring me closer?', 'Am I doing this as service to others or does it come from ego?' When I ask myself these questions and check in with my intuition, it helps guide my actions.

When I aligned myself to service to others rather than ego, my life changed greatly. Having the dream house and the big car and focusing on the acquisition of material things can come at a price. Nor does any of it necessarily make you any happier. This doesn't mean that you should live a life of poverty, though. However, allowing the universe to provide rather than chasing materialistic goals will ultimately put you in a happier and more aligned place with an enlightened sense of being rather than just existing from payday to payday.

At a particular point in my life there was a gap in my

existence that I thought I could fill with materialistic things. I also felt the need to please my father, to have a life and a career that would make him proud of me. I then realised that I needed to allow events to unfold rather than constantly chase them. I needed to step back from my ego self and allow the universe and the divine source to work their magic, and I enlisted the help of the Creator, the universal consciousness.

You have a unique purpose in life, and this is why you have been set upon this earth. You perhaps will never be a millionaire or invent a life-changing gadget, but you are here to fulfil a divine purpose. That's what we are all here for. Align your being with the divine source, enlist the help of the creative universe and allow events to unfold as if guided by a divine hand.

Soul's Purpose Summary

I'm a massive fan of Wayne Dyer. In his book *The Power of Intention* (2010) he sets out ten steps for living your life so that you align to your soul's purpose. I have summarised them as follows:

1. No one shows up by accident, not even you. You are infinitely connected to the universal consciousness. There is meaning to your existence. Know that you are here on purpose. Be in a constant state of allowing.

2. Live your life in service to others. Let go of the ego and help others along the way. If it is your purpose to be a mother, put all your energy into your children. If it's nursing, put all your energy into making people better. Make a difference to others and let the universe take care of the details. Put joy, love and

enthusiasm into everything you do.

3. Align yourself to your purpose. Have faith that the universe knows your purpose even if you don't. Know that your purpose will be revealed, and have faith.

4. Ignore what others may say about what your life purpose should be. Your loved ones may think that they know what is best for you. This is your life, not theirs. Listen to your own heart.

5. Remember that the field of intention will work on your behalf. The universe supports life. Know that the universe is endlessly abundant and is working in your favour. See it as friendly, not hostile. See it working for you, not against you.

6. Act as if you were living the life you were intended to live. Act as though you are living a purposeful life (this doesn't mean spending above your means). Treat obstacles as opportunities to test your resolve and to find your life's purpose. The loss of a job, an illness or any other mishap can be seen as an opportunity to move towards your life's purpose. Everything is there for a reason.

7. Study the lives of people who know their life's purpose and replicate what they do. Read about inspirational people you admire and how they were motivated to stay on purpose. There are many motivational speakers with videos and books about this subject.

8. Meditate to stay on purpose. Dyer recommended Japa meditation (meditating on the word 'God' or 'Aah'). Meditation, even for just a few moments a day, will set your intention. I meditate each morning

to set my intentions for the day ahead and I also take time to connect with divine guidance.

9. Keep your feelings and thoughts in line with your actions. Check your thoughts. If you are in disharmony it will take you away from your purpose. Keep your thoughts positive and harmonious.

10. Keep a state of gratitude. Be thankful for opportunities and obstacles. See everything from a perspective of gratitude: jobs, successes, people and failures. Everything puts you on the path of your life's purpose. You're here for a reason and that is to be purposeful. Be thankful. There is much to be grateful for.

This was adapted from *The Power of Intention* (2010) by Wayne Dyer.

These points summarise for me what needs to be done to align to your life's purpose and for it to manifest. It's not an easy task, but these little pointers help me stay on track and remind me what I should be doing. I hope they do the same for you.

Chapter Seven

The Importance of Gratitude

Each morning, as part of my routine, I take time to express my gratitude for all that is good in my life. I make it my mission to start the day grateful and happy. Make it a priority to start your day being grateful for everything in your life: the daily sunrise, the birdsong, the running hot water in your home, the house you live in, the abundance in your life, and your family, your friends and your daily routine.

Giving thanks in this way helps to naturally take away some of our burdens in life. Take some time to consider how you start your day. Do you start your day complaining, or do you start it in a positive way?

Every Monday morning I would complain to myself on the daily commute to work. I would say, 'I hate this. The weather's as miserable as I feel. I'd rather be doing something else. I wish I could win the lottery. I hate my job.' Carrying the burden of going to work and feeling resentful and unfulfilled left me feeling heavy.

But by changing my mindset to one of gratitude, my outlook became more positive. My job became better because I started the day less resentful. I smiled more, and people responded to me in a positive manner. My relationships began to flourish because of my new attitude. Life became easier, and in time I become happier and more abundant.

Now, I make it part of my daily routine to express gratitude for all I have in my life. I am thankful for my job, my home, my family, my car, which gets me from A to B, and the anticipation of a successful day ahead. I make it my mission to start the day grateful and happy. My mindset switch has changed my life for the better.

Expressing Gratitude

Start the day by being grateful for everything in your life: your shower in the morning, the daily sunrise, your health, your job, the food on your table, the weather, whatever money you have in your pocket, your family and your kids, even the journey to work. The list is endless. Doing this helps take away some of the burdens of life, allows you to be in a state of mindfulness, and assists in your being aware of the possibilities in the day ahead and life in general.

It's about taking time to notice and to reflect on the things that I am grateful for. I carry this habit throughout my day and always try to take the time to say 'Thank you,' to whoever gives me assistance, whether that be someone who helps me solve a problem, opens the door for me, serves me coffee, or generally any activity that I can show gratitude to the other person for.

People who regularly practise gratitude are generally more positive. They tend to possess more compassion and kindness and are less stressed (and as a result this in turn could even lead to their having stronger immune systems). Many studies have found that people who make a conscious effort to count their blessings tend to be happier and less depressed.

A recent study has shown that adults who participated in a gratitude letter-writing exercise experienced significant improvements in their mental health.

Take time to reflect on the happiness that being kind to someone has given you in the past, and also reflect on how grateful they were. Now think about someone who complains all the time. Which state feels better emotionally? Who do you think is happier? The person who is grateful and has a positive outlook on life, or the complainer?

Take notice if you engage in gossipy behaviour or complaining yourself. Distance yourself from it. If you feel you dwell on negative thoughts or engage in certain behaviours, prompt yourself to do a mindset switch to more positive thoughts and behaviours. Spend time in the company of people who are uplifting and positive instead of complainers and naysayers. Sometimes it's easy to forget and slip into poor behaviours. But once you get into the habit of changing your behaviours and mindset it becomes easier.

Expressing gratitude for what we have, rather than concentrating on what we don't have, can bring about feelings of peace and generally a happier outlook on life. It will also change the mood of others around you to a mood that will be more in keeping with your own. When we focus on what we don't have it brings about feelings of frustration and angst.

When we are grateful, we can also begin to cultivate the ability of attracting more into our lives. This is the universal law of attraction. When we complain and are in a state of ungratefulness we put up unconscious blocks to receiving more. The law of attraction works like this: what you put out you receive back.

Gratitude Is an Element of Success

Gratitude is a vital element of success. Being positive and grateful attracts positive energies and experiences in our everyday lives. Gratitude can bring more meaning to your life. It can help you feel happier and more positive, and can help eliminate negative thoughts and ideas.

Studies have found that people who regularly express gratitude are generally more positive. They are also less stressed, happier, less depressed, and they usually have greater compassion towards others. Gratitude helps to develop a positive and more successful mindset.

Making a conscious effort to express gratitude will change your life for the better. It could improve your health, as you will feel less stressed, and could help you have more positive and fulfilling relationships too.

Appreciate all you have in your life. Gratitude has a role in the element of success, as being positive and grateful attracts positive experiences while simultaneously helping to eliminate negative thoughts and ideas.

When we complain it creates unconscious blocks to manifesting and receiving more abundance. What you put out you receive back: again, this is the law of attraction.

Be grateful, even for the things that don't go right. There may be a purpose to them, even though at the time you might not see it.

When I look back at some of the blackest times of my life, I see a purpose to them. They helped me to cultivate patience (something I don't have a lot of), put me on the right path in life, cleared away the old for the new, made me more resilient and helped me to develop the strength I've needed to get through whatever life throws at me. I constantly affirm that everything is divinely guided. I believe in divine timing: that things, people or situations arrive in your life exactly when they should do. There exists a divine consciousness, a divine structure behind all life. Instead of putting up a resistance to it, work with the flow of life rather than go against it.

One of the simplest and easiest ways to express gratitude is to say 'Thank you,' to others. The words 'thank you' can mean so much to the person you say them to.

At the time of writing, we are in the midst of the Covid-19 pandemic in the UK. Each Thursday evening at 8 p.m., the television programmes pause, and the whole country is encouraged to come out onto their doorstep, no matter where they are, to applaud our NHS workers and other key workers as an appreciation for all they do. It's an uplifting and encouraging act of appreciation. Although many NHS staff or keyworkers may not see our united act of clapping, the energy behind the act and the uplift it gives everyone who participates is tangible. It's quite an emotional experience. The people we are clapping for aren't physically there, but the key workers, knowing that everyone is out at their doorstep clapping, showing their gratitude, find it encouraging. For me it's been a moving experience to see my neighbours out doing the same ... to hear the applause, fireworks and hooters going off in the distance, appreciating the NHS and the key workers for all they do.

Giving thanks can make you happier. Gratitude is given in appreciation of what we receive, whether it is a gift, a service or a gesture of kindness. With gratitude people acknowledge the good in their lives. Making a conscious attitude to express gratitude can change your life for the better, make you happier, and help you have more fulfilling relationships as well as improve your health. It can also help to curb materialism, as it can lessen the desire to accumulate or to hang on to stuff we don't need, and consequently it can help make us less self-centred and selfish.

When individuals express gratitude they may see that there is a goodness in their lives that lies outside them as an individual, for example, a gratitude for the natural world that surrounds them. As a result they feel they are giving thanks for it being there and connecting with something greater than themselves.

Even when things are not perfect, gratitude reinforces the notion that there is goodness in our lives. People connect with something greater than they are as individuals, such as a higher power at work in the world, the air we breathe, the sea, or Mother Nature in all her glory.

Gratitude encourages a more positive outlook in life and helps to establish a more optimistic viewpoint. It can therefore reduce negative emotions such as envy, greed, resentment and regret.

Expressing gratitude in the workplace is good for morale and can help improve the performance of your co-workers.

Showing gratitude can give people a sense of belonging, combat feelings of isolation or loneliness and increase empathy for others.

Wayne Dyer famously said, 'If you change the way you look at things, the things you look at change.' In the past I used to get up in the morning and tell myself how much I hated my work. I knew I had to change my mindset and the script I was constantly repeating to myself. Instead of putting up resistance to my work in actively hating it, by changing my thought processes I worked with it rather than against it. My attitude to work changed, and I was happier and more successful at my work as a result.

Keep a Gratitude Journal

Studies have shown that writing down everything you are grateful for in a journal before retiring to bed will give you a better night's sleep.

Write down everything you are grateful for daily. Cultivating gratitude as a daily practice will bring you peace of mind and contentment, and will help elevate your vibrational energies. Be thankful every day, and thank others too. However, make sure that what you write has detail and so is not repetitive. For example, you may write that you are grateful for having spent time in your garden that day. Explain why. Detail exactly what you are grateful for. You could detail the relationships you are grateful for and why, the opportunities you have been presented with that day or something great that has happened. Several of my friends on social media participate in an online initiative of one hundred days of happiness, whereby they dedicate a hundred continuous days to post online what they are grateful for each particular day. Some of them like it so much that they carry on for the whole year.

Expressing gratitude takes you away from the repetitive inner dialogue that leads you away from happiness.

Cultivating an attitude of gratitude as a daily practice will improve your life and help you be happier, increase your sense of well-being and improve your relationships.

Stay engaged in a state of gratitude in your daily activities and see for yourself how it can make positive changes in your life.

Make it your mission to be grateful.

Chapter Eight

The Power of Positivity

We are, in essence, the sum total of our thoughts and the stories that we repeat over and over in our heads. We are the product of our upbringing, of our social and economic status (class), of our education and of the influences of friends and family. If we have been brought up by a family where we have been continually told we are no good, useless or stupid, we carry those influences into our adulthood.

So how do we develop the practice of being positive and optimistic in attitude, thought and deed, when perhaps the stories we constantly tell ourselves in our head are the opposite?

Developing a positive mindset can give you more confidence and success, improve your levels of happiness and improve your health by reducing the likelihood of developing depression, hypertension and other stress-related disorders. You can bring more power, health, happiness and joy into your life by learning to unshackle the hidden power of your subconscious mind. You already possess this power. Everything you need is already within you. You just need to learn how to use it and then apply it to all areas of your life.

It is the world within that makes your outward world. There exists a frequency match between the inner (mental) and the outer (physical) worlds. What we project to the outer world is what we manifest back. If we live in an inner world of fear and want, our outer (physical) world will manifest the same. It is the world within your thoughts, feelings and internal imagery that makes the outer world in which you live.

Great thinkers and creators in the past had the ability to tap into the powers of the subconscious mind in order to create great inventions, paintings and literature. You have the same ability within you. Negative and limiting beliefs will restrict you from achieving your full potential, whereas using affirming and positive thoughts will help you to expand your potential. Choose your thoughts every day, the same way you would choose your clothes: be the best version of you.

There is always a frequency match to the inner and outer reality in life. Therefore, if we project out fear, fearful experiences will be projected back. What we project to the outer world is what we manifest back. This is the law of attraction. Never use the words, 'I can't do this,' or 'I can't afford that.'

Norman Vincent Peale said, 'Change your thoughts and you change your world.'

Practise Thinking More Positively

If you have a negative outlook or are in the habit of continually having negative thoughts, it will take time and persistent effort to change those thought processes. With practice and consistency your self-talk will start to shift to that of a more positive and optimistic nature. Some days you will get up and feel in a fantastic mood, some days you will get up and feel not so great, and some days you will get up and be unable to get motivated. It's human nature to have fluctuations in moods. The more you train yourself to think positively, however, the easier it will be to maintain a positive outlook, even in times of stress.

Positive Speech

The first step towards positive thinking is to practise positive speech, as how we speak influences how we think. The more you repeat something the more it becomes embedded in the subconscious. This is how mantras work. Mantras are words or phrases repeated over and over, which then become embedded in the subconscious mind. If you tell yourself every day that you hate your job, or that every day is going to be a bad day, then that is what you will believe and that is what will then manifest. Instead, repeat to yourself how grateful you are for your job and that this day is going to be a good day. It does work.

Human emotions ebb and flow like the tides. Sometimes there will be good days, and some days you will experience setbacks.

The same is true with positive outer speech, not just inner speech. My grandmother always said, 'If you have nothing good to say then say nothing at all.'

Speak of others in a way that you would like them to speak about you. Don't engage in limiting beliefs with people. Engage instead in uplifting conversations. The same is for gossip: try to distance yourself from it. Steer clear of negative responses in social interactions: this includes social media and online activities. Use supportive language rather than being critical, judgemental, spiteful, unkind or hurtful. Be aware that you don't mirror the behaviours of others around you if those behaviours are negative. Come away from the conversation. Make a conscious shift towards speech that is more compassionate and understanding of others.

Actively choose to be happy. Getting rid of habitual negative thinking isn't immediately easy, but with consistent determination it can be possible. Sometimes you may slip back into negative thoughts or words but the more aware you are that you are doing it, the easier it will become in training yourself back into positive words and thinking.

Establish a Morning Routine

A positive morning actually starts the previous night, before you go to bed. Why? Because your morning mindset and initial thoughts upon waking both start invariably with the last thought that you went to bed with. Make a conscious effort to instil positive thoughts and a positive mindset in the last five minutes before switching the light off.

My husband's grandmother always told us that the secret to a good relationship was to never go to bed on an argument. Such good advice. The thoughts you go to bed with, especially if they are bad ones, will probably churn over and over in your mind throughout the night. It is imperative that the last few minutes before sleep are calm and peaceful, to help you get a good, restful night's sleep.

When you awake, take quality time each morning, around fifteen to twenty minutes daily, to start your day in a positive way.

Have your journal to hand, perhaps by your bedside,

and take time each morning to write down the positives to each day and the things you are grateful for. Expressing gratitude for what you have can make you feel happier and gives you an uplifting start to the day. Take time to read a passage from an uplifting, inspirational book. I have several books by my bed from which I can read a short passage for a minute or so to start my day with a positive vibe. There is also a wealth of apps available for your phone to provide inspiration for the day. I have a Wayne Dyer app from which I can read an inspirational passage that contains a positive message for the day. Some people may like to read scripture to start their day to give them motivation and focus. Whatever you choose is individual to you.

Spend some quiet time thinking about your day ahead. I always take a few moments of quiet contemplation to think about my day and what I have planned. If tasks or activities come to mind I write them down so I don't forget them, and I ruminate on the day's activities, from my journey to work, to meetings, to my journey home, to my evening's gym classes. I actively visualise my day beginning and ending positively. So, for example, if I do have a meeting that day, I visualise positive outcomes from it.

If you have a lot to accomplish in a day, make a to-do list. This will organise your thoughts. It will set the day's focus, help accomplish your goals, and free your mind from the clutter of thoughts.

See the Good in All Situations

An unfortunate part of life is setbacks and disappointments. There's a common saying: 'When the going gets tough, the tough get going.' When you've actively pursued and tried to instil a positive attitude and mindset, it's vital not to let life's knocks set you back. Try to see the positives in every situation and look for the silver lining in every cloud. If things are so bad, remember that they will soon pass. I believe that things are put there for a reason: trust in the process of life and how it may be guiding you to something better. Challenges can be seen as an opportunity to learn and grow and to develop character. Develop faith in yourself, faith in your abilities and faith in life itself. A relative once said to me, 'Once you hit rock bottom, the only way is up.' She was right. At the time when she said this it was one of the lowest points in my life, and I knew that if I could get through that I could get through anything.

When things get difficult, let go of past events as you cannot change them. All you ever have is the present moment. And, if you change your thoughts and attitude in this moment, you will change the future into a more positive one. Instantaneously.

Forgive Others

Forgiveness starts with the self. If, like me, you spend hours beating yourself up for every misdemeanour in life, take heart. Forgiveness is a choice, and without making mistakes you would never learn. We learn by our mistakes. A lack of forgiveness, for ourselves and for others, robs us of our happiness and can make us depressed and anxious. Practising forgiveness contributes to your overall happiness and is a key step towards living a more balanced and positive life. It gives you peace of mind. Hanging on to bitterness and resentment leads to unhappy lifestyle choices and a whole host of other problems, particularly with relationships and making connections with others.

Making a conscious, deliberate decision to let go of anger, bitterness and resentment is the first step towards freeing yourself from the prison of your own mind.

Forgiving is not about forgetting or condoning the actions of others, but it is about coming to terms with what has happened and moving on.

Take action steps towards forgiveness by first making a list of all those people you need to forgive (you may choose to do this in your journal). This list may also include things you need to forgive yourself for.

As you write your list, write down how each individual has caused you pain. Identify what they have done to you to cause you to feel this way. Now, make a conscious effort to practise forgiveness for each person. It may help you to actively surrender it to the universe, to God or to another higher power, one which is greater than you. Take conscious steps to forgive each person in turn. The act of forgiveness is your gift to you. You will no longer be a prisoner of that person's actions.

Sometimes talking to others may help. This may mean seeking counsel in a trusted friend or counsellor or perhaps speaking directly to the person who has hurt you. Be positive in your endeavours, but do bear in mind that the objective of this exercise is to actively forgive the other person, not cause more resentment or harm.

Forgiveness will ultimately take time. It is unique to each individual. Learn to show compassion to others. Put yourself in the other person's shoes. Perhaps you need to ask yourself if you are to blame in any way.

See yourself free of resentment and anger and seek to find that forgiveness, however long it may take. Use a visualisation and affirm that you will fully forgive this person for any misdemeanours, and release them. Every time this person comes to mind, state to yourself that you forgive them and let them go. In time the person or experience will fade away, until eventually you will think of them or it no more.

Building a New Blueprint

The word blueprint is used in home building: when you build a home the architect creates a blueprint of what your new home will look like. We can apply this term to the mind. What does your mental blueprint look like? Is your blueprint constructed of fear, doubt, worry, want and limiting beliefs?

Put a concerted effort into building yourself a new blueprint: one of abundance, creativity, joy, peace and harmony. By reconstructing your blueprint to include these thoughts rather than limiting ones, you can express your full potential and create the life you want. By concentrating on good thoughts and not dwelling on the bad, your subconscious will begin to accept your new blueprint and bring to fruition a new mindset and life experiences.

Use your new blueprint to heal relationships, to attract a new career or a new partner, to improve your health and to free yourself from disharmony.

Positive Affirmations

As we have discovered, we are the sum product of our schooling, of what our family and friends have told us, and of our social and economic environment.

We may have been constantly told that everything

about us is less than perfect. We carry these thoughts and experiences into our adulthood, repeating these ideas over and over in our mind and therefore creating mental blocks. We can change these persistent recordings in our head into positive thoughts and actions by turning negative self-talk into positive self-talk.

The use of positive affirmations can assist in changing our mental programming. This can be an effective tool in creating an abundant life, in self-healing, in establishing a harmonious relationship and in creating abundance.

Look at a specific area of your life you wish to improve. In this case it may be your health. An affirmation could be, 'Every day in every way, I am getting better and better.' This affirmation can be applied immediately and can be used for many different areas of your life, such as better health, better relationships, being better at work, and being better at achieving your sales target.

Whatever affirmation you choose it can be written in your journal, typed up, or perhaps painted or drawn. The choice is yours. Put it someplace where you can see it, focus on it and repeat it daily. Positive affirmations can assist in keeping you focused on the results you wish to achieve, and, with constant repetition, you can eliminate any doubtful feelings you may have.

Consistently used, positive affirmations will make subtle changes, although they may not happen overnight. Consider that you are putting your affirmations out into the universe, and the universe is conspiring to put things in place in order to fulfil your desires. A kind of cosmic ordering service.

Make sure the affirmation is concise and is stated as a fact in the now. Don't use a past or future tense. State it as if it is happening now. For example, state, 'I am getting better,' rather than, 'I will get better,' or alternatively, 'Today is going to be a good day,' rather than 'Today will be a good day.' If you find yourself short of funds, assert to yourself that money is on its way to you rather than stating, 'I don't have…', or 'I can't afford…'

Moving Through Fear

Feel the fear and do it anyway.
—Susan Jeffers

How many events in life have caused you fear? How many times have you turned down opportunities for fear of the outcomes?

Many fears hold us back in life, but fear is a natural part of life. It's part of our ancestral make-up, the inner checking mechanism that our ancestors had in order to perceive whether a situation was dangerous or life-threatening.

Confronting our fears and overcoming them is an essential part of our path. It can sometimes take courage to live your life in a way that perhaps others don't understand or maybe even disapprove of, and fear may be an element or an emotion that you need to overcome. This could be the fear of the unknown, a fear of what people will think, a fear of how things will progress in the future, or a fear of change.

However, fear can also arise in situations that are unknown to us and push us outside our comfort zone. Fear in general life, particularly fear of failure, fear of things not going to plan or fear of what people might think of us, can really hold us back from achieving a fulfilling and rewarding life.

Over the years I've had to confront many fears and really push myself to overcome them and tackle things or events that would have been so easy to say no to, and I could have just stayed in my comfort zone.

This past year, I've had to really push myself to explore new ways of working and putting myself out there in ways that I would never have done before, and it's not been easy.

It's the scenarios that you build up in your head, the nagging voice that says, 'You can't do that. What will people think? You haven't got the ability or the resources. No one will be interested. What happens if it fails?'

There is the need to assert yourself and say, 'I can do this,' rather than 'I can't,' when thinking of situations that may push you outside your comfort zone. Yet once you have pushed yourself through the situation or event, the statement probably changes to, 'Why did I ever doubt I could do it?' or 'What a great experience. I'm so glad I did it.'

It's the fear of failure that stops us from taking those action steps and causes us to step into a negative mindset, rather than looking at what the positive outcomes may be. The great thing is that once you conquer your fear and go ahead with whatever it is that causes those doubts, afterwards you will know that if ever that event or situation arises again you will be able to get through it successfully. Even if things don't work out the way you planned, you will learn by your mistakes.

When things go right the experience will build character and confidence, and give you the knowledge that you have the ability to be able to tackle those challenges whenever they come your way again.

Try looking at things differently. What would happen if those events or scenarios you feared actually made a difference to your life and changed it for the better? Or what if you developed a new skill that you could take further or share with others? What would happen if you went through those fearful events and positively changed your life or the lives of others around you for the better?

It's very easy to say no, so much harder to say yes. What would you say yes to? How would it enhance your life, move you forward? How stuck would your life be if you said no to every opportunity that came your way?

Try visualisations to see yourself in your mind's eye as unafraid. Play the scenario in your head and run through not what could go wrong, but what could go right. See yourself as confident and courageous. When the event happens, feel and act as if you are confident. Stand up straight, smile, and act with confidence.

When faced with fear, be aware of all the facts but maintain a belief in a positive outcome no matter what the circumstances. If you feel fear taking over physically, take a few deep breaths while reassuring yourself that everything will be just fine. Fear is usually the resistance that is felt when experiencing something that is new and unknown. So let go of the fear, assert that all is well and of love and of peace, and move through it. Dealing with fear is a part of life's journey. We must learn to walk through all fear and turn that fear into focused awareness.

Take some time to write down and look at which fears have held you back. What have you always wanted to do yet fear has held you back? Next, think about what would happen if you said yes and put those desires into action. Then plan your action steps and set into motion your desired outcomes to realise those dreams with confidence.

Chapter Nine

Goal Setting

Goal setting for many is something that they do at the beginning of the year as part of the ritual of those New Year's resolutions and the 'new year, new me' mindset. For many the start of the new year means starting off anew with promises of finding a better job, getting fit, losing weight, giving up a bad habit, saving, or paying off debts. Every year I would say to myself, like many people, the same thing: 'This year I'll lose a stone in weight, save money and cut down on alcohol.'

It's a fact that on average most New Year's resolutions fail after six weeks. We lose the motivation to stay on track and revert to the same old ways. In more recent years, I looked back on my life and tried to remember how I used to achieve goals. When I was younger, I always had a five-year plan of my life and achieved most of my aims. But eventually, as time progressed, I forgot to set goals, as my life began to move in different directions. Then I remembered how I always used to have a five-year plan, so I started setting goals again. I finally achieved things I didn't think possible and completed projects that I had been chipping away at for a few years. Now goal setting is part of my life, and with it I'm achieving great things.

Instead of setting goals at the beginning of the year, why not constantly set new goals and revisit ones that have been previously set? Effective goal setting identifies where you want to be within a specific time frame. It focuses on the results, identifies where you want to be and looks at where you are now. Setting effective goals gives you the route to how you want to get there, the steps you may need to take and the resources that you will require. It can translate into daily activities that you need to perform to move you towards your goal. Goals don't just have to be for the year. They can be more short-term as well, such as monthly goals.

Goal setting is something that I do regularly. I set myself clear goals, which I focus on regularly, revisit and rework as necessary. When I wrote my second book, I wrote specific goals with a clear time frame in mind, which helped me keep my focus and helped me complete my book within the time parameters I set myself.

Goal setting is an important tool for success. Goals create a focus for where you want to be in life. By setting goals you can give more emphasis and focus to achieving certain things. They don't have to be materialistic. They could be spiritual, such as joining a church or developing a spiritual practice. Or they could be emotional, such as being more present and calm. Or they could be physical, such as getting fit.

What are your goals for today, for next month, for one year from now, for five years from now or even for ten years from now? Goal setting is another tool in the toolbox of conscious manifesting. Successful people set goals. Setting goals directs the attention and gives you something to work towards. Goals give the focus towards the dreams you have. They give direction, something to strive for and ultimately self-satisfaction when the goal is achieved. It's only a dream until you write it down. Then it becomes a goal.

Goal Setting Steps

Here are some pointers to set you off.

- Goal statement.

  What is your goal? Identify it. Be specific and make it time-constrained, in that you set a date for the goal to be completed. Remember, this can be revisited if things don't go to plan.

- Why is this goal important to you?

  Identify why the goal is important.

- Action steps you need to put in place to achieve your goal.

  List the action steps you need to take. Break the big picture into small steps. Set a time by which you wish to complete each action step. For example, can the action steps be taken immediately? In a month? In a year? Or are they ongoing?

- Skills and resources needed.

  What skills do you need to achieve your goal? What resources do you need? List everything you need.

- What obstacles may I face?

  Identify the obstacles that may hinder progress. A lack of money or resources? Maybe it's an emotional block such as fear. Identify them.

- How can I overcome these obstacles?

  Now look at how you can overcome those obstacles. What do you need to overcome the obstacles? Improve your skills? Generate more clients? Do you need less procrastination or fewer distractions?

- My reward when I achieve my goal.

  Set yourself a reward. There is no greater joy than in realising a goal, which in turn builds self-confidence. Plan a reward, no matter how small. It will give you an incentive.

There are lots of resources that you can access online, especially personal goal setting sheets.

So, write those goals down. Revisit them regularly. Make new goals when the old ones have been achieved. Rethink and revise goals if they don't seem to be working out.

Setting goals can be a wonderful tool which can help give focused intention to your desires and subsequently help you achieve great things in your life.

Visualising Goals

Mindfulness and taking time to tune into your desires and what you wish to focus on can help in setting goals and tuning into what you really desire at a soul level as well as what serves your current purpose in life.

Sit in a quiet space, take a few deep breaths and still your mind. Now place your attention on your innermost desires. Connect with your inner being and explore what inner desires you wish to manifest. Visualise how they would enhance your life and well-being. Explore which feelings come up as you visualise and tune into how they make you feel. Once you have desires that you wish to manifest, write them down. Then take time to set those goals within a time frame and the steps you are going to take to achieve them. Revisit your goals regularly and rewrite them accordingly, as some may take longer to achieve than others, or in time circumstances may change in that those goals might no longer serve your purpose.

Creating a Vision Board

A vision (or dream) board is a collage of images made up of what you wish to manifest in your life. It works with the law of attraction, in that it focuses your thoughts and puts out to the universe what you wish to manifest in your life. It is designed to be a source of inspiration that can be looked at daily, to inspire and motivate you to achieving the goals you have set yourself or wish to manifest.

Putting up your vision board where you can see it every day will give you an automatic way of affirming what you want to manifest in your life.

Vision boards are collections of images and perhaps phrases that reflect what you envision your life should be or what you want to achieve. For example: a new kitchen, a new home, happiness, family unity, career success, a beautiful garden, or a holiday.

Vision boards can be drawn using lots of images and colour, pictures from magazines or catalogues, or images printed from the Internet.

By making a vision board you are creating a sacred space that displays what you want in life. Visualisation is a powerful tool to use in manifesting desires. When you create a vision board and display it in a place where you can see it often, you are creating a visualisation experience whenever you cast your eyes upon it.

A vision board should focus not only on what you want but also how you want to feel. The more your board focuses on how you want to feel, the more energy is put into your vision and the more likely it is to come to life. My vision boards contain images and words about how I want to feel, such as happiness, peacefulness and joy. I have my boards on display where I can see them every morning.

Making Your Vision Board

Anything that inspires you can be put on to your vision board. Areas to cover may be relationships, finances, health and well-being, the home, spirituality and personal growth. There is no need, however, to cover all these areas. Focus on areas that have meaning to you. You can put personal statements and positive affirmations on your board (there are lots of resources you can find on the Internet to help you). There is no wrong or right way to create a vision board.

To make your vision board consider using the following:
You will need a corkboard (these can be picked up from any good stationers), or a poster board or a large sheet of card. You'll also need glue, sticky tape or pins for sticking items to the board, as well as coloured pens or pencils. Many images can be printed from the Internet, as well as phrases, sayings, positive affirmations or inspirational quotes. Images to be used can be cut from magazines or catalogues. Above all, be creative.

The most important thing is to set time aside in which to create. Personally, because I follow the phases of the moon, I like to create my board around the time of the new moon, as this is considered a potent time to set intentions.

Set aside one or two hours when you won't be disturbed so that you can use all your focus. Make yourself comfortable. Lay everything out before gluing or pinning it on to the board. I like to cover my board so that there are no spaces. If you want you can put a picture of you in the middle, to remind yourself that this is for you. You may wish to include close family members as well. Most of all, be creative and let the ideas flow.

When you've finished, display your vision board in a prominent place where you will see it every day.

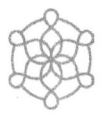

Chapter Ten

Journaling

If your life's worth living, it's worth recording.

This is a quote from Tony Robbins, a hugely successful business coach, inspirational speaker and entrepreneur.

Having kept journals and diaries for most of my life, I know how the act of journaling and writing down my experiences and thoughts has helped me over the years. It's a habit that I've had since I was twelve years old and I still have my first journal. I wrote in it at a very difficult time in my early life.

As a solitary child I recorded my experiences, good and bad, and somehow it helped me. It also helped me process the pain I felt as an adult when I looked at my journals years later. When I was a young adult, although I didn't realise it at the time, my journaling developed into goal setting, and all my objectives at that time were successfully achieved. I got a new job and a new relationship and gained my independence. Each goal was achieved step by step, as I had laid out in my journal. Little did I realise at the time that I was using techniques that would help me further on in life. At that time of my life I also started five-year plans, setting down all I wanted to achieve in the next five years.

Journaling is a tool that can help tap into creative processes and, as I know from experience, can be used to set goals and intentions. Journaling is useful in helping create a focus for successful creative endeavours.

The act of writing uses the left, more analytical side of the brain. While the left side of the brain is occupied, it leaves the right side of the brain free to create (the right side of the brain is for creativity and the arts). Subsequently, writing or journaling can help bring clarity to situations, solve problems and help release blocks to creativity, and can also help with the formulation of new ideas. It allows you to gain clarity on issues and assists in working through problems.

There is no magic formula to successful journaling. It's unique to each individual. You don't even have to write formally if you don't want to. You can adapt a variety of techniques to suit you. You can use drawings, doodles, make lists or use mind mapping strategies.

Journaling can help on so many levels: emotionally, physically and spiritually. You don't even have to be good at writing to be able to journal. When I was teaching young adults, I recommended that they kept a diary or journal to help improve their literacy skills.

Journaling is recommended by therapists as a powerful way of developing a deep understanding of your mind and emotions, and it can assist in developing self-awareness. When someone is more self-aware it helps in developing their sense of well-being by cultivating well-adjusted, grounded and balanced feelings and emotions. It can also go some way in developing a more positive attitude and increasing feelings of happiness.

Studies have shown that writing about events that are emotional and even traumatic can improve both the psychological and physical health of the participants.

A study showed that employees who spent fifteen minutes at the end of the day writing about how well their workday went had a more improved performance at work, compared to those who didn't journal. The study indicated that reflection led to better performance.

In qualifying as a teacher, a journal was kept for me to reflect on my initial teaching sessions, and to evaluate what went well and what didn't. This journaling process helped assess how to improve my lessons and how students responded to certain activities so that I could formulate how to structure future sessions. It helped me evaluate what did and didn't work.

The Medium

Whether you choose to write your journal on paper or via a digital format is a personal choice. Neither is a better or a worse option. Personally, I like a good-quality, aesthetically pleasing, hardbacked journal for the job, one with a ribbon in it so that I can easily flip over to the next page. Pens are also important for me, as I like ones that are of a good quality, flow well and are not too scratchy.

Language

It's good to go with the flow when journaling and not worry too much about spelling mistakes or grammar. However, it is worth noting that journaling is good for developing communication skills and writing fluency, and it can help you become more comfortable with general writing skills.

Time

Be consistent with your journaling practice. Try to do it at the same time each day if you can. This helps develop a regular habit. I like to journal at the end of the day, but some people prefer first thing in the morning and some prefer last thing at night. However, it is a personal choice. Just go with the flow and do what feels right for you. Try to keep the time spent manageable. Fifteen minutes or so is enough.

Privacy

Your journal is for your eyes only. In it you can feel free to explore your deepest thoughts and feelings. The more securely you can store it, the less inhibited you will feel and the more you will explore the depth of your emotions, especially if you are writing about a very personal or traumatic event that you wish to keep to yourself. If you journal electronically, keep your writing protected with a password.

Reflection

Reflection, to me, is the important part of the journaling journey. It helps you look back at past experiences and what you have learnt from them. It also shows your journey from the place where you once were to where you are in life today, and how far you've travelled and developed as a person. It can help you identify important points in your life and can assist in developing strategies for the future. By being reflective, it can not only help you identify plans that need revising but can also record your successes and help formulate ideas for the future.

If you forget to journal, catch up when you remember. Try to make it a daily habit and, above all, be consistent.

Chapter Eleven

Harmonious Relationships

How people treat you is their karma; how you react is yours.
—Wayne Dyer

When I undertook my teacher training, one of the things we had instilled in us was that no matter how good a teacher we were, no matter how much effort we put into our teaching, we would not please everyone all the time. We were encouraged to just do our best.

It's an unfortunate fact that when it comes to relationships and people that's all we can do – try our best – for no matter how much you try to get along with others there will always be someone who will criticise you, dislike you for no reason or make judgements about you. Once you accept that you can't please everyone, you can go a long way in deepening and easing the relationships in your life with the people you make a connection with.

Having been a people-pleaser all my life, it was learning the lesson that I couldn't please everyone, no matter how I tried, that was a game changer for me. It revolutionised my life. Until then, I had tried so hard to please everyone.

Learning this fact on my teacher training course helped me to teach confidently because as a teacher, students may just dislike you for no reason other than you're a teacher and a person in authority. People may just dislike you because of no reason other than they can, or because you will never be good enough in their eyes.

Establishing harmonious relationships can be difficult, even with the best of intentions. I was born to two parents who had multiple relationships and marriages. As a result I became withdrawn and isolated as a child and had great difficulty establishing friendships and building relationships with people. As an adult, I had to learn (sometimes the hard way) how to develop and sustain true friendships and to learn how to make worthwhile relationships with others. Because of all my childhood experiences, I suffered from abandonment issues and a lack of trust in others. I literally had to learn to be sociable and also how to talk to people. It took me a long time.

Even now there are times when I become withdrawn and find it difficult to be sociable. Marriage for me has also been difficult and I wouldn't say that it's been an easy ride, but my husband and I will be celebrating thirty years of marriage soon. Marriage, like life, is a series of ups and downs, and bumps along the way are inevitable. Learning to navigate those difficulties is the key to establishing successful relationships.

Problems in Communication

Problems usually begin when communication breaks down, which is something I've consistently seen through my parents' various relationships. When things are difficult, it's good to first sit down and have a frank discussion.

Modern lifestyles have taken their toll on family life and the art of talking to one another. Varying working patterns, distractions, such as the television, online activities and gaming, and not sitting down together to eat, have all eroded some of the times that families can spend together and talk to one another.

There is currently a campaign here in the UK called 'Britain Get Talking', which highlights the need for people to talk to one another and share problems, as people in society are becoming more and more isolated. This has been evident in the Covid-19 crisis, where people have literally been unable to interact with others due to the lockdown and the mental health of many people has suffered as a result. The campaign (and others like it) has sought to highlight mental health issues, with the emphasis on being able to talk and how essential it is for keeping mentally fit and healthy.

Talking to your children is also vitally important. Having come from a dysfunctional family and then in later life working with challenging behaviour in young adults, I have learnt that sitting down and talking through problems is the first way to try and resolve issues or nip them in the bud before they escalate. This is of course, a generalisation, as many people go through many different experiences, but sitting and talking through issues is a starting point for many.

Resolving Conflict

Unfortunately, as we navigate through life, we can't always avoid conflict, try as we may. So when we encounter conflict it needs to be looked at as an opportunity to grow, and as a learning curve. Communicating honestly with the other person is the first step to resolving conflict. If you experience difficulties with a person close to you, make contact with them and arrange to meet at a neutral place such as a cafe, coffee bar or other public place. If you live with the person you are in conflict with, sit down over a coffee together in a space where you won't be disturbed or find somewhere out of the home to sit and talk, such as a park bench.

Meet them on a one-to-one basis. Don't go mob-handed, or the other person will automatically go on the defence and feel that you're ganging up on them. Sit down and start with a compliment – something positive, nothing too heavy – such as saying that they look well.

Start the conversation by stating that you are sorry it has come to this, and that you are having this talk to resolve the dispute and to have a frank and honest discussion about it. Put your point across, and when it is their turn really listen. Be aware of your body language and give each other space to talk. If you jump in, mid conversation, to put your point in, you're not listening. Let the other person finish what they have to say. Try and establish how you will fix things. Conflict resolution is a two-way street. It needs cooperation and a little bit of give and take. Develop strategies to put in place to halt any further conflicts so that you can get along more harmoniously if possible. Be aware of each other's boundaries and expectations.

This is a generalisation and will not solve all conflicts. It will depend on the seriousness of the situation, but it gives some pointers of how to potentially come to some resolution with others.

Relationships and the Law of Attraction

We are all interconnected, as we all come from the same source: the divine spark, the universal consciousness.

We emanate a particular energy field, and as a result we attract people who are a match to our particular energy or vibration. Everyone we interact with and develop a relationship with is a vibrational match to our own. The people in our lives are a reflection of who we are. This is the law of attraction: what we put out we receive back. If we are out of alignment with the source of energy, of our true nature, we attract into our lives people who are also out of alignment. If we have been brought up to feel unworthy, we may attract partners or develop relationships with people who also make us feel unworthy. If we respect ourselves we will attract people into our lives who respect us in return.

If a person comes from an emanation of love they will equally attract loving experiences into their lives. If a person who constantly moans and complains tries to find a loving partner, the energy they give out may block their ability to find that loving person they so desire. By being in a state of moaning and complaining and not coming from a place of love, they will not attract the loving experience they want. It all starts from within. How can you love others if you don't come from a place of love or indeed love yourself? A person who complains and moans will end up only complaining and moaning about their relationship and find fault at all levels.

Be clear about what you want to attract. If you wish to attract a happy, fulfilling relationship, connect with the deep knowingness within you that the right people are out there and put it out to the universe that this is what you want to attract. Know that the universe is conspiring to bring the person/people into your life. Be willing to receive those loving people. Check in with yourself that you are ready and really willing to attract those experiences. If not, is there something that is holding you back? Be what you are looking for. Emanate that energy. You are a co-creator of your own reality. Trust that everything is in divine order and that everything will show up in divine timing. Know that the universe has your back and is conspiring to bring what you want your way. Tune into that vibration. Don't doubt it or engage in depleting self-talk.

Every experience, even a bad one, gives you the tools and strength you need to develop and grow as an individual. Bad relationships have the ability to show you exactly what you don't want. Learn from them. Everything is for a reason. There are no mistakes, only lessons.

Everything shows up exactly when it needs to do. This is divine timing. Make sure you are a vibrational match to your desires. Start by loving yourself, for without self-love you truly cannot love others around you. You can't make demands on this timing or argue with the universe. You may have to exercise patience for a while, but in the meantime hold on to those desires that you wish to manifest without forcing. Be sure in the knowledge that everything will show up when it should do and not before. Sometimes it may show up in a different way than you expected. By putting up demands you block progress. Instead, surrender to the progress of divine timing.

To Love Oneself is to Connect to the Divine

Love is all there is. Everything else is illusion.
—David Icke

There are no greater words than 'I love you.'

Love is the essence of divine power. It is the bond that binds us together with friends, family and lovers. In the words of Alfred, Lord Tennyson, *'Tis better to have loved and lost, Than never to have loved at all.'*

To love others, you must also love yourself. Love brings us back to the source of all that is and all that can ever be. The greatest essence there is on this earth is love: the love of your partner, your family, your companions and your pets. Extend that love outwards and love will be reciprocated to you.

When you see people and step in, judging the way they are or the way they look, take time to reflect that they are part of the divine source – the same as you. Remember that no one is imperfect, as we are all perfect in our own imperfections. Look to replace those thoughts and bring them back into alignment with the divine. When you judge others, perhaps you are also judging yourself or are reflecting other people's previous judgements of you. Take time to check in with those thoughts and turn them to love. Take time in surrounding yourself with love and loving thoughts.

When you judge someone to be fat, dirty or unkempt, or look down on them because they are not the same as you, take time to reflect that those people have had experiences in their lives that have brought them to the point where they are today. Seek to find opportunities to replace judgemental and limiting thoughts with love and compassion.

Replace contemptuous thoughts with those of love and compassion through connecting with the heart centre.

Love is all around us. We just need to see it, to tap into it. Love is a magnificent force that can change people's lives beyond what they ever perceived possible. Love is the glue that connects us, holds us together.

Love begins with you, as your physical body is a part of the divine source. It is beautiful and perfect, so treat it as sacred. Tend to it with care. Make improvements by nourishing it with healthy, wholesome food. Purge it of toxins and give it some self-care. Express the radiance of abundant love through every pore of your being, from inside out. Express your being through the act of love. Feel it radiate outward, and sense it coming back to you in droves.

Your soul is your garden. Tend to it daily and feed it with love.

Chapter Twelve

Stopping Repetitive Thoughts

We have as many as forty thousand to sixty thousand thoughts going on in our minds regularly, on a daily basis. Many of those thoughts will be made up of repeating past scenarios in our mind, or worrying about the future and events that haven't yet happened. Many people find themselves in a constant cycle of repetitive and negative incessant thinking.

Over the years, when talking to people, I have found that many people, particularly but not exclusively women, end up in a cycle of playing out scenarios in their minds. This is repetitive (sometimes obsessive) thinking and constant worrying, which whirls around and around in their heads.

It's something that I can closely relate to, having spent many years worrying over small things and playing out scenarios in my head, situations that to all intents and purposes never (thankfully) materialise.

However, when we are in a cycle of thoughts that we can't let go of, this can lead to obsessive behaviour, worry and anxiety. Obsessive thinking can lead to exaggerated and irrational worries, can disrupt sleep patterns and can lead to compulsive behaviours.

Coping Strategies

If you're worrying about a certain scenario, a technique that can help is a visualisation exercise. Let's use, for example, a past argument or a falling-out which you got into that you keep replaying over in your mind.

Stop and take a few moments to do this. Visualise the scenario and then freeze the frame from the scene, like you would when watching a show or film on your TV screen. Now, take out all the colour, and turn the scene to black-and-white. Next, shrink the image until it's really small. Then, finally, visualise yourself crumpling it like a piece of paper, then throw it away.

Another strategy to take us away from repetitive thinking is concentrating on the breath. This can help in distancing us from or disconnecting us from our thoughts. To do this you can use the breath as a focus to home in on invasive thoughts when they take over. The constant stream of thoughts can be reset by taking a pause and simply focusing on the breath.

Take a breath in slowly, in through the nose and out through the mouth, and put focused attention on to the breath going in and out slowly. By doing this your awareness is brought away from thoughts to the breath, leaving those thoughts to fade into the background. This helps calm the physical sensations behind the emotion of the thoughts and allows the thinking to become more rational, therefore helping to make better judgements and responses.

I like to visualise the negative thoughts being released as I breathe out, and see the thoughts disappear like smoke into the air. This method can also be used in a form of meditation in order to pause and reflect on repeating thoughts or situations.

Find a quiet space to meditate in silence. Drawing in a few, deep breaths initially, at the beginning of the meditation, can help release and let go of thoughts, worries or concerns.

An extension to this is focusing on the present moment. Eckhart Tolle recommends bringing the attention to the breath, while simultaneously accepting the moment and letting go. Eckhart Tolle suggests that you should recognise that the past has happened, so it cannot be changed. And the future hasn't arrived, so it's a waste of time thinking about what may or may not ever happen. All you have ultimately is the now, the present moment, and you should bring the attention to the present moment in conscious awareness by taking deep breaths and asking yourself how you are feeling now, at the moment.

Alternatively, journaling can help, by getting your thoughts down on to paper or on an electronic device. However, if the thoughts that occur are about another person, be mindful that what you write is not actually sent to that person, for example by text or email, especially if you have thoughts of anger or are upset about a situation. For this reason, paper is much better, as long as it is kept privately or destroyed afterwards. By writing thoughts down you get the words out of your head (see the chapter on journaling).

Another technique is to give your thoughts a silly voice, such as the voice of a cartoon character like Mickey Mouse or similar (something that is non-threatening).

A further technique can be using an affirmation or mantra. A mantra is a phrase that can be said repetitively.

Any word or phrase can be used, but use something positive. This could be, 'Life is good,' 'I am better,' or 'Everything is OK.' You can always use singular positive words such as 'om,' 'peace,' or 'calm.'

Focus your thoughts on your chosen mantra. If your mind wanders, turn your attention back to your mantra, word or phrase. It can be repeated silently in your head or quietly to yourself. This can be practised at any time: while you are cleaning, out shopping, walking the dog or making your way home from work. Again, mantras can be repeated silently in your head, especially if there are people around and you feel self-conscious.

If you find that your mind is racing with repetitive thoughts, worries or concerns, you can do this next exercise to help take your mind away and bring in some stillness.

Take your thoughts to your hands. Think about your hands. Place your attention on to your hands and see if you can feel your hands without actually touching anything. Try to feel the energy within your hands. You may begin to feel a tingling or a warm sensation in them as you do this. Your thinking will slow down. If you wish to take this further, you can think about or tune into other parts of your body as well. Eckhart Tolle calls this exercise an anchor for the state of presence.

Colouring books, cooking, gardening, playing an instrument, walking in nature and exercise are all options for calming the mind and participating in activities to focus the mind away from repetitive thinking. All these strategies and activities can help move your mind away from obsessive, negative thinking.

Some thoughts that cross our mind may be totally inappropriate in real-life situations and we would probably never actually enact the things we think about, but inevitably for many of us they are there. We might suddenly get angry about a person and play out a scenario in our heads of actually punching them in the face or worse, even though we would never do that in real life. Some of these strategies may help get some of those destructive thoughts out of our minds and allow us to bring our thoughts back into alignment and overcome them in a more positive manner. Remember, it takes time to develop good habits. Be consistent, as it takes time to see results.

Ultimately, if you can't get repetitive, obsessive thinking under control, consult your healthcare professional so that they can treat any underlying issues effectively.

Chapter Thirteen

The Power of Prayer

Prayer is not an old woman's idle amusement. Properly understood and applied, it is the most potent instrument of action.
—Mahatma Gandhi

When faced with challenging times, for example, death, divorce, health issues, financial difficulties or any challenging situations, many people resort to prayer. Prayers may also be said daily for religious reasons, to connect to the divine, and for spiritual enlightenment. However, I do not believe you have to be religious for prayer to work, and that anyone, no matter what their religion or belief system is, can participate in the act of prayer. I know atheists who pray now and again.

Having been brought up in the Catholic faith (rather loosely), I always viewed prayer as the repetition of a standard set of verses: Our Father, Hail Mary and so on, learnt off by heart and repeated parrot-fashion.

The act of prayer does not have to be of a religious nature. It can be a personal experience of connecting with the cosmos, the divine intelligence behind all creation.

How you interpret it is unique and personal to you. Prayer helps you make a connection to a higher power that is greater than you. Saying prayers changes the vibrational energy around you, instilling a more positive energy and one hopefully of connection.

Personal Form of Prayers

In more recent years I have found a far more personal form of prayer. It is not one that is set or is to be repeated diligently, but it is one that speaks intimately to a divine consciousness, an all knowing, all-encompassing source that will hear my intention. Some of you may call this God, Goddess or Creation.

This act of prayer for me is done quietly or in silence in peaceful meditation, and my prayer is sent out as a request to the universe to assist or to show me the way to deal with whatever issue or challenge I have. I hold it in my heart that there is a higher intelligence that knows ultimately how the prayer will be answered or how events will unfold, and will ultimately show me the way through with divine intervention. It is not a request but an acknowledgement that the answers to my prayers are on the way, and that I am grateful.

As a healer and as a reiki practitioner I have said many a healing prayer at the behest of those who have requested it. I belong to prayer groups on social media, where members collectively say prayers of healing on behalf of those who request it, be it to heal a pet, to heal a person of their ailments or to heal situations such as arguments, marital or relationship problems, the loss of a job, or to pray for the successful outcome to a situation.

Belief in Prayer

What I have personally found is that the prayers sent out have had wonderful results, including what could be considered miraculous healing against all the odds. These prayers really worked, not for everyone all the time, but for most. I've asked for prayers to be said for me for various reasons and have found that the collective energy of the prayers of the group produced results beyond my expectations and achieved resolutions to any challenges I was facing at that time on an emotional and physical level. It's not just the intention behind the prayer. I believe it is the combined belief and the faith of those praying, and the fervent belief held that the prayers will be ultimately answered in whatever way possible. And it is also for the highest good of those involved.

It's the relationship between the belief and the practice in prayer that is important. All the events and experiences of your life have happened as a result of the actions of your own thought processes. What you put out you receive back: as I've said before, this is the law of attraction. Therefore, belief in prayer is perhaps the fundamental principle in respect of how prayer may work. Prayer is the act of directing the conscious and the subconscious mind in unison, using the power of intention toward a desired outcome or goal.

By applying belief behind prayer and knowing that the infinite intelligence of your conscious and subconscious mind will achieve the desired results, and by expressing gratitude that the desired outcome will be achieved … this is the ultimate healing of prayer. Have belief that an infinite intelligence is behind all healing. You may not know what the ultimate outcome may be, but instil in yourself the belief that your prayers will be answered.

For example, a placebo is a medicine or procedure that has no apparent benefit for the recipient other than a psychological one. A placebo may work, therefore, simply because the person who receives the placebo believes it is genuine and that it will work. If you believe the effect strongly enough it will work.

Prayers don't just have to be said when things go wrong. They can be said as a point of gratitude. Gratitude is a very powerful antidote to life's challenges, a reminder to you that you have much to be grateful for. The act of gratitude can help make a shift in your attitude to life itself.

Prayers for Guidance

Prayers can also be said for guidance. I regularly pray for guidance, asking the divine intelligence, which I know exists, to show me the way, to show me how I may serve. If we sit still and ask for guidance, we may be clearly directed to the answers. For some, this may be similar to being given an answer intuitively. Personally, this act of prayer gives me the answer for direction in my life when I cannot see the full picture. The bigger picture may yet to be revealed and my prayer is to guide me in the direction I need, despite not being in full view of what is to become. Sometimes it takes patience to receive the answer I seek, but I believe that it will be revealed to me and that everything will fall into place perfectly.

It may take time for prayers to be answered. But know that the divine order of the universe is conspiring to make these prayers happen, however long it may take. It may be that you cannot see the full scope of the situation or event (a bit like when you are reaching the peak of a hill but can't quite see the views yet). But once you reach that point, the scenery may be revealed before you and you will be able to see the bigger picture.

So, in the meantime, hold the belief that your prayers will be answered, even if it is in ways that you don't expect.

Chapter Fourteen

Decluttering – Mind and Life

'A tidy house is a tidy mind,' a friend once said to me. How true that is. The two go hand in hand. Home and mind: the clutter we have within the home and the clutter we have in our mind. Over the years I've found it difficult to function properly within a home that is a mess. Throughout my working life I've also found that the most successful, motivated people I know are tidy and extremely well organised. If you're spending every Monday morning frantically trying to get ready for work and getting the kids ready for school, while trying to find clothes, socks, etc., in that pile of washing you've not organised and put away, and then trying to make up packed lunches at the last minute in an unorganised kitchen, holding back tears of frustration with knots in your stomach, you'll know where I'm coming from.

Clutter Can Be Stressful

A home that is disorganised and full of clutter can be a cause of stress and anxiety. A home that is streamlined, organised and clutter-free is not only more calming, but when you invest time in organising you ultimately free up time elsewhere and are more productive. When you are searching for items under piles of things that you haven't sorted or you don't know where things are, it costs time and effort and creates energy blocks and frustration. Personally I try to limit the number of shelves and knick-knacks I have in my house, as they seem to attract dust. Dusting takes time, and ultimately less is more: less time dusting, and more time to do other things.

Cleaning out the clutter helps streamline the home, creates space, reduces stressful living and promotes a more positive atmosphere. Holding on to material things and possessions makes your home less vibrant and makes the energy in the home stagnate. Decluttering creates space for more abundance to come through. It's a paradox: the more you let go the more you receive. Holding on to stuff blocks the energetic flow to life. A house that is overly full of possessions causes stress and frustration, and if it is like that it ultimately blocks the energetic flow.

Once the clutter of your home is dealt with, it will be easier to deal with the clutter of your mind and your lifestyle.

My grandmother was a prime example.

My grandmother was a classic example of someone who could not let go of possessions and who developed a hoarding habit. This, in essence, came from a sense of lack and of loss stemming back to her years during the Second World War in Britain when rationing was in place. She also lost people who were close to her. She held on to things that were no use: old papers, magazines, books, knick-knacks, junk, food containers, clothes and shoes that no longer fit her or were worn out, and she also kept food beyond its sell-by date. Things were stacked up in piles against her walls, and her cupboards were full to the brim. In many ways her hoarding was extremely wasteful. She would buy tins of food that she would not eat, and items from shops that she would never use.

The house became difficult to clean and manage. Eventually, one New Year's Day, she fell out of bed and was unable to free herself because she had become wedged between the bed and the pile of bedding and clothes piled up against the wall. After this incident (which could have been very dangerous) she agreed to start letting some of her stuff go. Her hoarding habit was unhealthy and taken to the extreme, but it shows how clutter can take over someone's life.

I've shared this story before, but it describes my first-hand experience of how people can develop a hoarding habit, and how much of an impact it had on our family.

Less clutter helps create a home that is easier to clean, is healthier, and is more energetically pleasing.

Devoting time initially to decluttering the home can result in a more positive, productive lifestyle and saves time in the long run because you know exactly where everything is without having to wade through things. And it will be easier to keep tidy.

Ways to Start Decluttering

Start by having a time dedicated to decluttering. Simply pick a room and start with a drawer. When that drawer is done, pick another drawer. Then pick another drawer or a cupboard. When the whole room is done, pick another room. Start small, one space at a time, so you don't feel overwhelmed. As the saying goes, 'The journey of a thousand miles begins with a single step.'

Think about how you feel when you walk into a home that is clean and free of clutter. Estate agents use techniques when they put a house on the market to promote a good, positive environment that has clean lines and is streamlined in appearance. You can feel the environment the moment you walk into a room on an energetic level.

Take time to let go of things that you no longer need, for example, books, CDs, DVDs, accessories, and clothes that no longer fit or items you haven't worn in the last year. Be ruthless. Whenever possible, recycle items or take them to a charity shop. I love those charity bags that come through the letter box that you can fill with items and leave outside your home for collection. You are not only recycling but also contributing to charity, and it's collected for you. Some charities will happily collect items if you ask them, especially large items like dining room tables or wardrobes.

Invest in space-organising items for your cupboards and baskets to put things in, for example cupboard organisers for the kitchen as well as wardrobe and drawer organisers. Cheap baskets can be used in cupboards, which can then be lifted out for easy cleaning. Things you really can't bear to part with can be put away in your attic or the garage, or in storage facilities and lock-ups.

In the spiritual sense, decluttering makes more room for manifesting the things that give you joy. Being organised and less cluttered is a habit of a successful mindset.

Decluttering can be a cathartic experience. You can feel a sense of joy at having less stuff. And you will have cleaner and simpler lines in the home and more space.

Some Strategies

Some pointers for decluttering:

- Try not to set aside an entire day to declutter, as this may cause a feeling of being overwhelmed. Eight hours of trying to declutter and get organised is debilitating. This way you won't just give up. It's very easy to be overwhelmed by the task ahead so just do one thing at a time, whether it's one drawer or one cupboard.
- Start by picking a drawer. When that's done, pick another drawer. One drawer a time over a few days or weeks is better than none and will eventually pay dividends.
- If you regularly get charity donation bags through your door, make use of them. I love them. Best of all, they're collected for you. The hardest part is filling them up. Do check the information on the bags to see what the charities will and won't take, though.
- Give to charity shops. It's a type of recycling, plus you help good causes.
- Rome wasn't built in a day. Take one step at a time.
- Don't expect perfection. Don't expect your spaces to look like those in catalogue pictures.
- Set a space that is organised and fulfils your needs.
- In order to keep motivated, remember that being organised and tidy helps to complete tasks more efficiently and quickly. It saves time. You won't be trawling through junk to find that pair of scissors or that scarf.
- Be prepared to let go of stuff. You may never fit into that skirt you've been hanging on to for four years. If

it's not been worn for over a year, it goes.

- Invest in stacking boxes. I love the range called Really Useful Boxes, which are available from DIY shops and online. For those on a budget, pound shops also have handy cheap stacking boxes and baskets for organising cupboards, etc.

Remember, no one is perfect. My Achilles heel is books – I can't part with them. But do try to give things up with grace and with gratitude. A tidy home is indeed a tidy mind.

If decluttering your home is too much for you there is help available out there, including trained professionals who can help clean and declutter homes that have overwhelmed their owners.

Decluttering the Mind

Decluttering doesn't just apply to the physical environment. It applies to the mind as well. Meditation can help declutter the mind. It can release stressful thoughts, and in doing so can assist in bringing in clarity and peace. Journaling can declutter thoughts by putting them down on to paper.

Reducing commitments can help streamline your life and raise your energy levels. Start by making a list of the commitments that you have in the course of a week and look at each one in turn. Are there some personal commitments that you can delegate or share with other members of your family? Are there commitments at work that you can delegate to others or seek help with? Do you need to say no more often? Could you get up earlier to get things done? Do you need to organise your time more effectively or be more productive with the time you have?

The world is full of distractions. Consider what can distract you during the course of the day. A good example is social media. Do you really need to know what Betty has had for her tea?

Constantly watching television programmes that give no joy, watching television for the sake of it or playing endless hours of gaming activities instead of getting on with the things you need to do are other examples. Keep up to date and check what you need to, but don't let distractions take your focus away from what needs to be done.

When you engage in decluttering your life of not just physical things but also unnecessary activities you will probably find yourself less stressed and more organised, and you will free up valuable time. Your energy levels will probably be better as a result, and you will feel more in control of things.

Chapter Fifteen

The Miracle of Early Mornings

There's an old saying that my grandma used to say to me as a child: 'The early bird gets the worm.'

I came across *The Miracle Morning* by Hal Elrod and Pat Petrini a few years ago through a friend who had a network marketing business.

I've had an interest in mindset strategies for many years. The use of positive affirmations to change the way I think and go beyond the limitations of my mindset, goal setting, meditation and organising my space have all had their place in making my life more productive and happier. They've helped me live my life in a more positive way, helped in my progress and helped me achieve goals that I set myself.

The concept is simple: get up early in the morning and get things done. This came as a revelation to me. It's a simple idea but one I'd never really thought of, as until then I had dismissed my grandmother's sound advice.

Successful, happy individuals follow daily routines and habits which help keep them focused and able to complete tasks. Setting aside each day for me, connecting with the divine source and thinking about the day ahead has been a valuable daily routine, one that I have followed for many years. Meditation, reflection, setting positive intentions, reading something positive and expressing gratitude for the things I have, all contribute to my early morning activities that set me up for the day. Because I have this routine I feel happier and more fulfilled.

Setting aside time each morning and thinking about the day ahead gives you the opportunity to look at what needs to be accomplished that day, to consider which resources and tools you may need, and also gives you time to collect your thoughts. Making a list, if necessary, is also part of this routine, as it takes away the stress of having to remember things and gives mini goals to accomplish throughout the day.

From working in education for many years, I've experienced at first hand the need to be focused and highly organised, especially when dealing with the heavy, demanding workload and the tight deadlines that teaching brings. When I completed my teacher training, the course tutor stated very clearly that in order to succeed at teaching we had to be highly organised. Worse still, we were warned, if we weren't, we would see the end of our close partnerships.

Over the years I've seen many tutors crumble under the pressure. The most successful and inspiring tutors, though, it seems, were always the highly organised and focused ones, the ones who got up early, got into work first thing, and got tasks done before the start of the day's teaching at nine that morning. Many of the tutors started their day at seven to seven thirty in the morning. With this extra effort of being in early they managed their time more effectively, didn't take work home (many other tutors did) and had more free time at weekends. They structured their day to be as effective as possible with their heavy workloads and were more successful as a result, and generally coped a lot better than their counterparts who came in late and were unorganised. This just gives an idea about how highly successful people work and the focused mindset that they adopt.

As I have evolved my daily practices over the years, I have put my efforts into starting the day with a positive mindset, as a good morning mindset for me is everything.

Many years ago, when my kids were small, I didn't have the luxury of devoting my time to my morning mindset, so many of the activities that I adopted then, such as my daily meditation practice, had to be done in the evening.

However, as the years have progressed, I've developed the habit of getting up earlier. It had an impact on my life, and resulted in my being able to get more things done and organise myself better. As I have developed this practice my mornings have organically evolved, in that I have developed a set routine of meditation, considering my mindset, making positive affirmations, and reading or listening to an inspirational passage prior to getting dressed and ready for the day ahead.

When I first read *The Miracle Morning*, I realised that I already had many of the recommended steps in place. I just had to push myself to get up half an hour earlier to complete additional tasks such as a small amount of exercise. I allow myself one day a week for a lie-in at weekend. I have established a regular routine for the other days of the week, regardless of whether I'm at work or not.

This has proved invaluable during the Covid-19 pandemic. My days are ordered, structured and constructive as much as possible, even though many restrictions have been placed on movement out of the home and the fact that I had a great deal of time on my hands due to my place of work shutting suddenly.

Many people have struggled with having so much time on their hands. This hasn't been the case for everyone, as most key workers have had even more work to do, and some retired essential workers have been called back to work. But, for many, the excess time on their hands has been difficult for people to manage, especially as the lockdown has rolled on for weeks with little let-up on the restrictions. No socialising, no restaurants, no visits to family, no trips to the seaside or favourite places, no going to the gym. Everything has been focused on staying within the home as much as possible.

Having a structured, organised day has been essential for many who have suddenly found themselves with so much time on their hands.

My Miracle Morning

This is my usual ritual each and every morning, that is except one day a week, usually at the weekends, when I take time to rest and take it easy during the course of the day.

At 6 a.m. each morning my alarm, which is tuned to the local radio station, as I like to wake up to music, wakes me up. Occasionally I rise at 5 a.m., particularly if I'm writing or have some other project to complete.

First thing I have either hot water and lemon with a little honey, or a green juice on an empty stomach before having any other hot drinks or breakfast. Hot water with freshly squeezed lemon wakes you up better than any caffeine.

The citric acid in the lemon helps detoxification, and it's also good for cleansing the kidneys. It stimulates the liver by encouraging the production of bile, which aids with digestion. The ladies who taught my yoga classes swore by hot lemon water first thing in the morning as the key to good health. Alternatively, I will have a green powder mixed in a little watered-down orange juice, again on an empty stomach so the nutrients can be absorbed more readily. Organic green powders come in various forms such as spirulina, wheatgrass, barley grass and various plant-based mixtures, and can be purchased from any good health food store. I always make sure that the powders are organic, as they taste a lot better. They are an excellent source of trace minerals and essential nutrients such as zinc, magnesium, iron and other vitamins, depending on the type of powder. It's a good way to get part of your five a day, especially if your diet isn't all that good.

Next comes my morning meditation. Meditation is an important part of my life. I'm a daily meditator, and have been for twenty years. I take a good twenty minutes to meditate. It helps me quieten the monkey chatter of my mind and clarifies my thinking. It sets me up for the day, and helps me find some peace and balance to begin my day. Meditation doesn't have to be complicated: just focus on the breath, and if your mind wanders bring it back to the breath.

If I have time, I like to stretch prior to my meditation practice by doing three rounds of sun salutes. Completing a few rounds of sun salutations or any other gentle yoga practice, I have found, is beneficial to my strength and flexibility and settles my mind ready for meditation, as I let go of thoughts and focus on my movements. The sun salutation is a range of yoga movements, and it originated in hatha yoga.

As a reiki practitioner and healer, at the end of my meditation practice I send out distant healing to my immediate family members and anyone else who needs it and who has given me permission to send that healing out.

During this quiet time after healing and meditation, I cast my mind towards the day ahead. In this time I do what I call 'colouring my path'. I visualise what I am going to do during the day. For example, the journey to work, a meeting that I may have and other things that I may need to accomplish during the course of the day. I colour my path with violet to ease my day ahead and to smooth my path. I visualise the colour violet on a straight road ahead of me, which is symbolic of my day's activities. The colour violet is considered a highly spiritual colour (it is the colour of higher vibration and calmness). Most days it helps, especially if I have a difficult meeting. But, as in all areas of life, sometimes things don't go to plan. Any challenges I face during the day are a reminder of an opportunity to grow and develop.

Once this is done, I go over some positive affirmations. I have these printed out and written on an A3 poster that I made that is pinned up by the side of my bed so that I can look at the affirmations each day and repeat them. I also make it part of my day to give gratitude for all that I have, such as my job, my car, my shower, my breakfast, etc.

I read or listen to an inspiring passage, in a book, on an app, on my phone or online. My favourite inspirational authors are Wayne Dyer, Eckhart Tolle or Helen Schucman, to name but three. I also have a collection of books that contain inspirational passages from philosophers and sages through the ages for quiet reflection.

After all this, I have breakfast, shower and get ready for my day. It sounds a lot to pack in at the start of the day, but some of the above activities can take just a few minutes and are easily incorporated into a regular routine.

My main exercise is done in the evening when I'll go to a gym (pre the Covid-19 lockdown) and participate in group sessions such as spin classes or HIIT (high-intensity interval training) classes. The evening is also when I take time to do my journaling. Some people prefer to do this in the morning, but for me, my journaling practice is part of my reflection at the end of the day. As an avid goal setter, I will take time to set goals if needed, even if this includes just making a simple to-do list. This activity helps take things out of my mind so I won't worry about forgetting anything the next day.

My phone is put down and I try not to touch it after 8 p.m., nor do I look at it prior to my meditation practice. The blue light that mobile phones give off stimulates parts of the brain and can supress melatonin, which can affect the internal body clock (the circadian rhythm). As someone who struggles to sleep, I need all the help I can get. So for this reason I make sure I don't touch my phone, as it can affect my ability to get a restful night.

Miracle Morning Practices

In his book *The Miracle Morning* Hal Elrod details his six-step routine to help kick-start the day. This was created with the idea of taking your own personal development to the next level in mind, and to start the day in the best way possible: calm, focused and with plenty of energy to get through the day. He researched the most successful people and examined the daily practices they used, and from this he came up with what he calls Life S.A.V.E.R.S. (Elrod, 2015).

As I've said, I already had many of these in place in my early morning routine, but took the decision to get up an hour earlier to fine-tune my practices and ensure that most were implemented.

Life S.A.V.E.R.S., Elrod suggests, are designed to help you start the day the best possible way, so that you are focused and positive, mentally, physically, spiritually and emotionally, and ready to give your best.

They are activities that help start your day with the best possible mindset. The acronym Elrod uses stands for:

- Silence: ten minutes.
- Affirmations: ten minutes.
- Visualisations: five minutes.
- Exercise: ten minutes.
- Reading: twenty minutes.
- Scribing: five minutes.

These are simply a guide, and the list above is an example of the formula to use to begin the day. The times allocated for each activity can be altered, but as a general guide all the activities can take an hour in total. For me, silence or meditation takes up twenty minutes of my time, with reading ten minutes.

Silence

This is your time for stillness, and to breathe. As we've discovered, meditation is a fantastic tool for calming the mind, reducing stress and helping to establish focus. The simplest practice is to sit quietly and focus on the breath, allowing any thoughts that arise to just float away.

Alternatively, there are apps available to use on your device. Or you may just choose to use traditional prayer. The choice is yours.

Affirmations

An affirmation is a positive statement with a specific aim in mind towards an ultimate goal. It works on the mindset at a subconscious level to reprogramme negative and restrictive thinking. The statements you use should always be in the present tense, never in the past or the future, and they should be specific. Recite your chosen affirmation each morning, not parrot-fashion, but with emotion, conviction and belief behind each word. Make affirmations a part of your routine and read them daily, not just now and then. Consistency is key.

There are many examples of affirmations available online. You may wish to start your affirmation with, 'I am committed to...' then insert what your affirmation is. It may be, for example, doubling your income, increasing sales, writing a book, or losing weight. In the statements you make, include a specific time frame and a statement about why you want whatever it is, for example, to feel better, to provide financial security, or to help your family. Affirmations can be printed or written out, and then placed in a prominent position where they can be seen every day and recited each morning. Review your affirmations and change or update them regularly.

Visualisation

Once you have completed your affirmations it is time to take a few minutes to visualise. Use this time to visualise what you want, how you want your life to be. You can also use this time to visualise your day ahead. Perhaps you have an important meeting or a job interview. Picture these events as being successful and see in your mind's eye that everything goes well and that there are positive outcomes as a result. You may wish to visualise your trip, if travelling, and see it going smoothly and without trouble. Visualise everything going in your favour.

Exercise

A great way to start the morning is with exercise. It sets you up for the day. How you do that is up to you. I like to start my day with stretching and a bit of yoga. You may wish to jump on an exercise bike, use a rowing or a running machine, or go outdoors for a run. Exercise in the morning will increase your energy levels for the day and will elevate your mood, while reducing stress levels.

Reading

Read something inspirational or motivational each day. There is a wealth of inspiring written material out there. Read a short piece to inspire your thinking and motivate your mind. Or you may choose to read from religious texts.

Scribing

This is another term for writing or journaling. I personally prefer to journal at the end of the day, but journaling in the morning can help set your mindset for the day ahead and focus your thoughts. It may lead to gaining valuable insights or those 'aha' moments. It also helps to articulate goals. Or you may wish to just make a list of things you need to get done.

Many of these activities are explained in more detail throughout this book. This is an example of how all these things can be put into an hour at the start of the day. Just an hour. At first it may seem a little bit daunting, but with practice and consistency it will get easier to incorporate these activities into your routine. Just setting your alarm an hour earlier in the morning could put you on the route to achieving fantastic goals as well as putting you firmly on the road to success.

Chapter Sixteen

Coping in Challenging Times

This book came about during a very challenging time of our social history – the Covid-19 pandemic. It has seen us here in the United Kingdom and other countries around the world in total lockdown. For many people, they have been isolated away from their families and restricted in many ways, including social interaction and freedom of movement. Things that we took for granted have been stopped, for example being able to hug our loved ones, being able to spend time with friends and family, including family members who we don't cohabit with, being able to go to the gym, and being able go to the pub and socialise or go out for a meal. We are not allowed to travel to our favourite places for a well-earned break. We have to keep away from beauty spots and we are not supposed to participate in sport, walk further than thirty minutes from our homes more than once a day or be out exercising for more than an hour. We can't have a massage, get our hair cut or go for a beauty treatment either, or indeed nip to the shops for anything deemed non-essential. We have always taken all these things for granted.

The stress of home schooling children while simultaneously working from home has proved a nightmare for some families. More distressingly, families have been unable to be at the bedside of those dying, and funerals have been limited to ten people or fewer. All places of worship have been shut and weddings have had to be cancelled. Tragic events have kept unfolding on the mainstream media while people at home have been praying that none of this would happen to them. People have been dying alone in their homes.

We were told to stay at home, but for many that has brought a great number of benefits. We have not had to go to work yet have still been getting paid, we have been spending quality time with the loved ones we live with, we have been able to catch up on all those jobs that have been neglected, we have spent lazy days binge-watching box sets or just being out in the garden. And we have been meditating, connecting with our true nature, as well as being able to devote time to self-introspection, creating, writing, learning new hobbies, baking and catching up on our reading.

There are winners and then unfortunately losers in all this. So many have lost their lives, and some families have been decimated. Loved ones have been unable to see their relatives in hospital and say their goodbyes, and nurses and doctors have been working around the clock to save lives. These are the real heroes: the key workers, the shop assistants, the postmen, the lorry drivers and the binmen. The time of the pandemic has seen the lowest-paid workers doing the highest-value jobs.

We have a new superhero in the form of a ninety-nine-year-old gentleman called Captain Tom, who, by walking 100 laps of his garden, raised in excess of thirty-three million pounds for the NHS and inspired a nation through his efforts. And every Thursday evening at 8 p.m. we would go out onto our doorsteps and clap for carers, NHS workers and other key workers. Never have I felt so much emotion and pride. Fireworks are let off, horns sounded, and wooden spoons banged on the bottom of pans.

But we have been stripped bare, exposed, and left vulnerable by an unseen microscopic enemy.

Even a simple task such as shopping for groceries has proven difficult. We have had to stand six feet (two metres) apart, while queuing outside major stores, patiently waiting to go in. The supermarkets have been operating a 'one out, one in' system, and we have not been allowed to shop together as a couple or as a family but have had to use trollies in supermarkets individually. Although currently food and household supplies are being replenished in the shops, in the initial weeks of the lockdown it was difficult to get hold of basics such as toilet rolls, painkillers, chicken, bread, flour and packs of beer, to name a few items, due to an initial surge of panic-buying. Trying to get your groceries from large supermarkets, only to get there and find the shelves stripped bare, was a shock.

On the other hand, many of us have had time on our hands, which we have used to create home-cooked meals from scratch, bake cakes and create things in the kitchen we've never had time to make until the lockdown. Although many have been left struggling for money, particularly the self-employed, many others have saved money due to the restrictions. Personally, I've come to realise how much money I used to fritter away on incidentals and unnecessary trips to the shop for bits. Being forced to think about trips out to the shops and having to plan my shopping and only getting what I actually need has been a money-saving game changer.

We've been stripped down to the core and the reset button has been pushed. The world appears to have been standing still for a while. And it stopped quite suddenly, it seems. There has been very little traffic on the roads, streets in towns and cities have been deserted, and there have been very few, if any, planes in the sky.

Where we live we are directly under the flight path to Manchester Airport. It is hard to express the sheer joy we've had, looking up at the clear blue skies with no contrails criss-crossing them, and being able to examine the night skies, which hold the stars, distant planets and the moon so clearly now. Our view has been unimpeded.

During the lockdown we were blessed with such good weather, which was unusual for rainy, dreary Manchester. The birds seem noisier and busier than ever, and some towns have had deer, sheep and goats roaming freely through once busy streets, as if investigating where all the annoying humans had got to.

Watching interviews on television, coming live from the homes of celebrities, politicians and prominent people, with their living spaces in the background, has been a revelation. For a naturally nosy person I've just loved looking at the backgrounds and imagining what sort of homes they are. There have been some choice selections in home decor. Some are stylish, some are awful. I have seen pop stars playing live sets with messy beds in view, and members of royalty coming live from a room that has dusty shelves in the background. Half of humanity has had to stay indoors. Never before has the world shut down like this. No one has escaped the reality of a lockdown, whether it be the wealthy, the famous, the rich or the poor.

It's been a journey of almost imposed self-reflection and introspection and re-examining life, its meaning, what actually matters and what needs to change. We have had to ask questions about what is really important. Is it the latest designer gear, the latest technology, having nice nails and getting smashed in the pub at the weekend? Or is it the simple things, such as a hug, closeness with those special people in your life, visiting loved ones in their home and having a coffee and a chat? Or is it being allowed to roam the countryside freely, explore nature fully or travel to coastal towns and beauty spots?

Throughout all this I have truly learnt how much I have taken for granted, and, although I didn't think I was, how materialistic I've been. I understand now that the material things really don't matter. I've learnt so many things about myself that I never knew, and have so many demons to confront. I have found a deeper spiritual understanding, a deeper connection to God.

I send out healing to the universe every day and have prayed like never before. I have connected to a deep level of understanding of my own nature and thought deeply about how we as humans have caused so much pollution and hurt Mother Nature and the Earth. Throughout this lockdown, it is believed that global warming could have been put back years, possibly even ten to fifteen years.

Through this period of isolation, deep reflection and inner as well as outer stillness, I have developed strategies for coping. I've had many of these strategies for some time. Some are obvious, but I've had to really lean on them and develop them further in these unusual, transformational times.

Coping Strategies for Stressful Times

- Panic and fear fog the mind, which can lead to irrational and fearful thoughts and actions. Try to keep positive and take a few deep breaths if you feel panic coming over you.
- Limit your exposure to television. We now have access to the news all day, every day. Most of the news stories are fear-based. Because people tune in, the adverts during breaks command the highest revenue. Fear-based news makes money. Keep up to date only with what you need to know.
- Focus on more positive things. Listen to positive podcasts, watch inspirational programmes, and watch positive online content. Take responsibility for your mindset and behaviours. Be present and be mindful.
- Don't catastrophise things in your head. And, if you start to do so, find something to focus on and take your mind away from such thoughts. It's OK to feel sad at times, but not excessively.
- If you feel panic and fear welling up, take a little time to take in some deep breaths to calm your nerves.
- If you can, take some time to meditate to still the mind. Focus on the breath or on an inanimate object, such as a cut flower or an apple.
- Take a walk, and if you can, take it out in nature or in a park. Walking can help alleviate anxiety and help instil more positive emotions and a sense of calm. Focus on your feet connecting with the earth as you walk.
- Focus on presence and being in the now. The past is gone. You can't do anything to change that, and the future is not yet here. All you have, essentially, is this

moment. If your mind wanders, bring it back to the present moment.

- Crystals. If you're sensitive to them they are great for instilling a little bit of calmness. Place your favourite small crystals in your pockets or wear one around your neck. (Worry stones work just as well. Choose a simple pebble, which you can take out and concentrate on for a moment or play with in your hand.)
- Essential oils are very calming. Burn some oils in a burner or place a few drops of essential oil in a bath, if you have one.
- Adult colouring books. When my children were small some of my happiest times were spent colouring in pictures with my youngest son, so I was overjoyed when adult colouring books came into being. The activity helps takes your mind away from overthinking.
- Look at your diet. This is more long-term, but changes can be made immediately. Look at eating more healthily, incorporating more high-energy, high-vibrational foods into your diet. Omit highly processed foods.
- Exercise. As above, a walk is good. Or a bike ride, running, skipping, yoga or any aerobic exercise that gets your heart rate up and that you can safely do.
- Journal. Journaling is wonderful at inspiring creative ideas and discovering solutions to problems.
- Reading. Read something inspiring and motivating or light-hearted.
- If you're at home for any length of time, like we have been during the Covid-19 pandemic, don't mope about. Be organised and motivated. Get up, get dressed, plan your day, do some work, create something or do some gentle exercise.

The one thing I've learnt throughout my life, and indeed more so since the Covid-19 pandemic, is that difficulties and challenges are put on your path to reveal your greatest strengths: determination, courage, resilience, strength of character and patience. There are lessons in every test we endure, and we learn the most when we are tested because we have the resilience to find the answers, which ultimately lie within our being.

Mother Theresa once said about the daily suffering she encountered, 'Every day I see Jesus Christ in all his distressing disguises.'

Appendices

Here is a selection of various meditations to practise in various forms. Some can be found in the meditation chapter, and others are meditations that have not been detailed in the main body of the book. They are all grouped here for ease of access, and are included to give variety and to take you further on your journey of self-discovery as you develop your meditation practice.

Appendix 1

Focusing on the Breath

(from the meditation chapter)

This is a simple meditation to begin with to focus on the breath. It is described in the meditation chapter but is also included in the appendices for easy access.

Find a quiet place where you will not be disturbed and sit comfortably. Close your eyes and take a nice, deep breath.

Bring your entire focus on your breath. Take a nice breath in. As you breathe out, visualise all the stresses and strains of the day melting away. Breathe in and see you are breathing in peace and relaxation. Breathe out all tension and worry.

Now focus on your feet for a moment. See them anchoring you to the earth, keeping you grounded. Now turn your attention back to the breath. Feel your chest gently rise up and down. Continue breathing normally as you relax. If your mind wanders, bring it back to the breath. Acknowledge any thoughts that may arise and see them float away as you continue to focus on the breath.

When you are done, bring your awareness back to your body. You may want to stretch. You may wish to focus on your feet grounding you into the earth. Be grateful for your experience and give thanks.

Appendix 2

Standing Tall Meditation

This can be found in the first chapter but is also included here in the appendices for easy access.

This breath work can be done standing tall like a mountain. Standing tall like a mountain is a common yet simple pose in yoga.

Stand with your feet in a comfortable position, hip distance apart. Drop your shoulders away from your ears. Take a few deep breaths and relax all your muscles as you breathe. Focus on the soles of your feet connecting you to the earth, grounding you. Now visualise a cord running up your spine, coming out of the top of your head, pulling you up tall and straight. With your spine erect and your shoulders relaxed you are standing strong, like a mountain, with the cord connecting you to the heavens above and the ground below.

Now bring your attention to the breath. Allow all thoughts to float away. Take a few moments.

When you are ready, bring your awareness back to the body. You may wish to wriggle your toes or lightly shake your hands to bring your awareness back.

This practice can literally be done waiting in a queue or at any time. No one needs to know you are doing it.

Appendix 3

Sitting Like a Mountain

Just like standing tall like a mountain, you can sit like a mountain. This exercise is good for those who have mobility issues, or indeed for finding a bit of calm while sitting at a desk, on a bench out in nature or sitting on the floor in a comfortable position.

Take a few moments to concentrate on the breath. Sit with your spine erect. Relax your muscles as you breathe. Let your shoulders drop away from your ears, relaxed. Bring your awareness to your body. Visualise a mountain. This can be a mountain you know, have visited or have seen somewhere. Have an image of the mountain in front of you. It may be rugged, jagged, have soft edges or a plateau. Perhaps it's grey and rocky, covered in greenery or snow-capped.

Bring the image of the chosen mountainscape into your body. Be the mountain. Your head may be the peak of the mountain, your shoulders part of its slopes, your lower body the bulk of the mountain. The base of the mountain is connected to the earth through the soles of your feet. Visualise the mountain. Sit and be the mountain.

When you have finished, bring your awareness back to your surroundings.

Appendix 4

Sitting Out in Nature

Sit quietly outdoors. Position yourself so that you can point your face up to the sky. Take a few deep breaths to calm your mind. Release the muscles of your body as you breathe. Let your shoulders drop away from your ears and relax. Then affirm for a few moments that renewed health and vitality is being drawn into your body from the universe or nature. Breathe it in.

When you are done, give thanks.

Appendix 5

Focus Meditation

This meditation is in the meditation chapter, but is also included here in the appendices for easy access.

This is a good way to meditate if you struggle to focus on the breath, as instead you place your focus on an object. You can use a candle and its flame as a focus, or you can use an object such as an apple or a flower.

Sit comfortably and take a few deep breaths as before. Visualise all tension leaving your body.

Now, bring your awareness to the object. Gaze at it with a soft focus. Do not think of words to describe the object. See the object without interpreting it. Now, close your eyes for a while. If your mind wanders, gaze at the object again. You may even see the object in your mind's eye. Let go of all thoughts and relax. Complete your meditation practice when you are ready.

Eventually, with practice, you will begin to be able to meditate without the object there. Remember, meditation is an acquired skill that develops with practice and patience. Your concentration will improve gradually.

Appendix 6

Simple Meditation Exercise

This is in the initial meditation chapter and is also included here for ease of access.

Find a quiet place where you will not be disturbed. Unplug the phone. Switch the mobile off. Sit or lie comfortably. I prefer to sit, as this way I know I won't go to sleep. If you are sitting, make sure your feet are flat on the floor. If they are not, place a cushion or a book under your feet. Close your eyes and take a nice deep breath.

Focus on your feet. Visualise roots sprouting from your feet, anchoring you to the earth and grounding you. Draw up through these roots the energy of the earth, which will empower you and help to clear away all negative energy.

Now begin to focus on the breath. Take a deep breath in. When you breathe out, imagine all the stresses and strains of the day melting away. Breathe in and feel that you are breathing in peace and relaxation. Breathe out and see all the tension and worries melt away.

As you continue to breathe in, imagine that you are breathing in a pure white light. As you breathe out, imagine you are breathing out a grey mist. The grey mist is all the tension, worry, problems and niggles you may have encountered during the day.

Sit in this peace for five or ten minutes. If your mind

wanders, bring it back to focus on your breathing. Focus on your chest, gently lifting up and down as you breathe. Focus on the beat of your heart as it pumps the blood around your body. Acknowledge any thoughts that arise and see them float away into the ether.

When you are done, feel at peace and fully relaxed. If you can, try to do this for twenty minutes daily. But remember that even five minutes is better than no minutes.

At the end of your practice, surround yourself with a translucent bubble to help seal in the peace and to protect yourself from negative emotions. Be of joy and positivity and give thanks for the experience. See the bubble expand fifteen feet below you, fifteen feet above you and fifteen feet from each side of you and fill it with love, light and peace.

Appendix 7

Meditation comes in many forms. The following meditation can be done in the same way as the previous one, but by using a candle instead. This is called a focus meditation. It may help you if you find your mind continually wandering.

Light a candle at the beginning of your meditation practice. Close your eyes. Use your breathing to breathe away tensions. See roots emerging from the soles of your feet and grounding you to the earth. Breathe in the white light of peace and positivity and breathe away the grey mist of stress and negativity.

When you are relaxed, open your eyes and gaze gently at the candle. Think of nothing else but the flickering flame. Soften your focus and hold the image of the flame. Close your eyes and allow nothing else to enter your mind. If your mind wanders, open your eyes and gently focus on the flame. Continue focusing on the flame, and then close your eyes for as long as you can. If you can manage it, aim for at least twenty minutes. Seal and protect your aura in a translucent bubble as before.

You may find this meditation practice easier than concentrating on the breath. Eventually, after doing this meditation a number of times, you will be able to simply visualise the candle.

As a precautionary note, please always take care with candles and make sure you extinguish them properly after use. Use candles safely and don't light them near curtains or anything combustible. You can also consider using an electric candle, but please be mindful of the environment if you have to dispose of it. In my mind natural candles are always the best, due to their natural light, but this is up to personal preference.

Appendix 8

Another type of meditation is the walking meditation.

While walking outdoors, bring your attention to your feet. As you walk, feel each footstep, one in front of the other. As you walk, imagine all the tension and stress of the day flowing from your body and leaving through the soles of your feet. Imagine the negativity that flows out of your feet leaving footsteps behind you, which transform into beautiful flowers. Breathe in the white light of peace and see the negativity continually flowing out of your feet as you walk. Continue in this way for as long as you feel necessary.

It is important while doing this meditation that you feel safe. I don't advise it near busy roads. It is a good meditation to do, though, in parks or in the countryside or even in your garden. Connecting with the outdoors and the earth is always good for getting rid of anxieties.

Appendix 9

Hug a Tree

During the Covid-19 crisis, the forestry commission in Iceland recommended that Icelanders should hug a tree once a day for five minutes. They cited the benefits of assisting in relaxation and to help with feelings of well-being. So hugging a tree may not be as kooky as it sounds. As a lover of trees, tree hugging when I'm anxious and stressed always makes me feel better.

Select a tree you feel drawn to. Try to pick a tree that is away from lots of busy pathways as trees that are set back from paths and are more secluded are believed to have greater energy. Stand either facing the tree, or if you feel self-conscious, you can lean on the tree with your back facing it. Either way, try to embrace the tree with your arms. Sense the tree with its roots, going deep down into the earth, then sense the height of the tree with its branches reaching high up into the sky. Really feel the tree and its connection to Mother Nature. Allow the tree's energy to take away all your stress and tension, transmuting it into positive nature energy. Stay there for about five minutes, or as long as you wish. When you're finished, give thanks to the tree.

Appendix 10

Listening to Inner Sound

This is a simple meditation best done at night and in a quiet room.

Sit in your meditation position comfortably. Take a few deep breaths to relax the body and calm the mind.

Now, turn your attention to your ears. Listen to the subtle sound in your inner ear. This is a faint internal sound. You will notice that each ear has a different resonance, a slightly different sound. Concentrate first on one ear and then on the other ear.

Let your thoughts dissolve into the resonance that develops. Do this for as long as feels comfortable.

Appendix 11

Tense and Release

Sit comfortably upright, or lie down. Take a nice deep breath. Hold it for a few seconds, then release it. Do this a couple of times.

Now turn your attention to your body, starting with your head. Take a deep breath. Scrunch up your face tightly, squeezing your eyelids and all the muscles in your face. Let go and release the breath.

Breathe in, tightening your neck and shoulder muscles, then lift your shoulders up and hold this position. Release and let go. Breathe out. Take a deep breath in and expand your chest and hold. Release and let go, breathing out. Take a deep breath. Suck your stomach in, while holding your stomach muscles in tightly. Breathe out, release and let go.

Now go to your arms. Breathe in, locking your arms along their whole length and clenching your fists, and tensing all the muscles in your arms. Hold. Breathe out, release and let go.

Now go to your buttocks. Breathe in, squeezing the muscles in your buttocks tightly and hold. Breathe out, release and let go. Now concentrate on your thigh muscles. Breathe in and squeeze and tense your thigh muscles. Hold. Breathe out, release and let go. Next go to your lower legs.

Breathe in, tighten your calf muscles, and pull your feet upwards. Hold. Breathe out, release and let go.

Lastly go to your feet. Breathe in, tense the muscles in your feet, curling your toes downwards. Hold. Breathe out, release and let go.

This exercise is good for releasing tension in the body. With practice it can be completed more quickly than when you first do it and it can be used as a prelude to a meditation or relaxation practice.

Appendix 12

Mirror Work – Self-Love

This is a practice I was introduced to by a midwife after childbirth, where I was advised to get a mirror and look at my changed body. It is a practice that perhaps you may feel uncomfortable with, particularly if you have insecurities about your body. We're pressurised as a society by images in the media of a 'perfect' body, whereas in reality many of us have what we may consider imperfections. Women, especially, tend to focus on what they consider imperfections rather than the beauty they already have. This practice helps with acceptance of your body, and with your self-esteem and self-awareness. In order to love others, we must first love ourselves.

Take off all your clothes. If you have a full-length mirror, stand in front of it. If you don't, use a large mirror or a hand mirror. Start by looking at yourself and holding your own gaze and sending yourself love. Then begin looking at every part of yourself. It may feel uncomfortable at first, but with practice you will eventually be able to look at your body fully with complete acceptance and love. Your body is you. Love and embrace it.

Appendix 13

Drawing Down the White Light

A more detailed version of this follows in Appendix 16 (the white light mediation). This is a shortened version to use when you don't have the time for a formal meditation.

The white light meditation is excellent at cleansing the aura, and the white light can be used at any time to cleanse away negativity in an instant. If you are in a stressful environment or are unable to focus, take some time out, even if the only quiet space you can find is in the loo. Take a few deep breaths and connect with the divine source. Visualise the white light and draw it down through the top of your head as you breathe in. Take a few breaths and breathe in the white light until you feel harmonised. Visualise it taking away any negativity and energetic debris as it leaves you feeling calm and centred.

The more you do this simple exercise the quicker you will be able to do it at any time and feel its effects.

Appendix 14

Colouring Your Path

This technique can be used to colour your path.

If you have an important meeting to go to or if you just want to set a positive path for your day ahead, as well as giving yourself protection from negative influences, tune into the violet ray to colour your path violet.

Sit in quiet meditation. Take a few deep breaths and visualise the day ahead and the tasks that need to be completed. Imagine that a there is a road or a path set before you. This road or path can appear however you like it (mine is always one straight road in front of me). Visualise the violet energy coming through and placing the violet colour on your path ahead. You could visualise, if you wish, a room or the place you are going to later in the day if you are familiar with it.

I have successfully used this technique time and time again, especially at work, when I know that I am going to encounter stressful situations, or when I am travelling to new places for interviews and so on. I also use it on my travels so that I may have a safe and stress-free journey. You can use this technique as part of your daily practice.

Appendix 15

The Auric Egg Breathing Exercise

This is a cleansing breath exercise to purify and strengthen the aura, the energy field around the body. This can be practised first thing in the morning upon awakening to prepare you for the day ahead, or it can be done at night to get rid of any negativity or stress that you have encountered during your day. In this exercise you are the yolk inside the egg.

Between the yolk and the shell are seven other layers. These are the layers of the aura, or the energetic field surrounding the body. This breathing exercise will help in cleansing and strengthening the aura.

On the in breath visualise that you are breathing up the back of your body from the backs of your feet to the top of your head.

On the out breath visualise the breath going down the front side of your body, sweeping under your feet.

Do this circular breathing from back to front seven times. Each time, visualise that you have moved slightly away from your body in an ever-expanding circle, until on the seventh breath you are at arm's length away from your body.

Then breathe up the left side of your body from the sides of your feet up and over your head.

On the out breath breathe down the right side of your body, sweeping under your feet.

Do this circular breathing from right to left seven times. Each time visualise that you have breathed the aura slightly away from your body in an ever-expanding circle, until on the seventh breath it is at arm's length away from your body.

Visualise yourself with a cleansed auric field like the shape of an egg that surrounds the body.

If you wish you can alternate between back to front and then left to right, breathing seven times in each direction.

Appendix 16

White Light Meditation

Find a quiet place where you will not be disturbed. Sit in a comfortable position. It is better to do this meditation sitting upright rather than lying down, as the energies will travel through the top of your head and through your body. You may wish to burn a candle and perhaps also some incense.

Close your eyes. Take a deep breath. As you breathe in, imagine breathing in peace. On the out breath, breathe away all tension and anxiety. Breathe in peace and love. Breathe out all tension, stresses and strains. As you breathe in, imagine all the tensions of the day and any thoughts and fears melting away with the out breath.

Continue to breathe in and out in this way until you feel calm and relaxed. Now begin to imagine a pure crystalline or white light six inches above your head. This white light is pure and full of love and peace.

Breathe in this white light through the top of your head. As it enters your head, feel it melt away all thoughts and fears, leaving your mind still and peaceful. Breathe out.

As you continue to gently breathe in and out, feel the white light moving down the back of your head, making your head relaxed. Feel the white light moving over your eyes and face, making all your muscles relaxed.

As you continue to breathe, feel the white light now moving down your neck, through your shoulders, making them relaxed. Now feel the light travel down your arms as it travels down your fingers and thumbs, taking all tension with it and leaving your arms feeling relaxed.

Now take this light from your shoulders down through your spine as it travels through your trunk, relaxing all the muscles and organs as it goes through your body, front and back.

Feel the light now travel down over your hips, through your thighs, knees, calves and ankles and out through your heels, leaving your whole body calm, relaxed and at peace.

Feel roots now, growing from the soles of your feet, down into the earth, anchoring and grounding you. Feel these roots grow and expand deep into the earth, like the roots of an oak tree, firm and strong. As you visualise these roots going deep into the earth, see that they find a crystal and that the roots wrap themselves around this crystal.

Now draw the pure energy from the crystal back up through the soles of your feet, through your ankles, calves, knees and hips.

Feel the energy from the crystal move up through your trunk, stomach, chest and internal organs as it travels up your spine to the base of your head. Take the energy of the crystal across your shoulders and down through your fingers and thumbs.

Now feel the crystal energy move up through your head as it moves to your crown. Feel this energy flow out through the top of your head as it now begins to flow outwards, filling your energy field with pure, crystalline energy. Feel it filling and expanding through your energy field at arm's length all around your body.

Sit in this energy feeling peaceful, relaxed and healthy for a few minutes. If your mind wanders at all, focus on the gentle rise and fall of your breath.

Now begin to bring yourself back to centre. Feel the streaming of the white light disconnect. Feel yourself sitting in the chair. Move your fingers and toes and feel aware of your surroundings.

When you feel ready, seal and protect this wonderful energy within your own energy field. Clench your fists and imagine a sphere of protection fifteen feet below you, above you, in front of you, behind you and at both sides, all around you like a huge translucent bubble protecting you and keeping you safe. To finish, if you can, reach down and put your palms on the top of your feet to ground yourself. If you can't reach that far, just run your palms down your legs as far as they will go. Stay there for a few seconds, then sit up and open your eyes.

Appendix 17

The Chakra Colour Meditation

The chakras are considered to be energy centres situated within the body's etheric field. Each chakra is associated with a colour and there many different chakras, but in this meditation we will concentrate on the seven main chakras. Each chakra is a spinning wheel of energy. The seven chakras are: the root or base chakra, at the base of the trunk, the sacral chakra below the belly button, the solar plexus chakra above the belly button, the heart chakra, the throat chakra, the third eye chakra, situated between the eyes, and the crown chakra, situated at the top of the head.

Find a quiet place to sit where you will not be disturbed. Turn off the phone. If you wish you can light a candle, burn some incense or put on some soft music. Do whatever makes you feel happy.

Sit with your feet flat on the ground. Close your eyes. Take a few slow, deep breaths. As you do this, start to connect with the universal white light of the divine consciousness. Breathe in this white light as you have done before, in the white light meditation.

Visualise a shaft of pure crystalline light coming down from the cosmos and entering the top of your head. See it engulfing your body inside and out, leaving through the soles of your feet, cleansing all negative energies as it travels through your body.

When you have breathed in the white light, concentrate on the soles of your feet. See roots like those of a tree sink deep into the earth, grounding you.

See the energy of the earth move up your body as it reaches your base chakra, situated in your perineum. Breathe in the colour red. As you breathe in the colour red, see your chakra become balanced with a red hue. If you see any muddiness or imbalance, breathe it away.

When you are ready, take the energy up to the sacral chakra, situated below your belly button. Breathe in the colour orange. As you breathe in the colour orange see your chakra become balanced with an orange hue. If you see any muddiness or imbalance, breathe it away.

When you are ready, take the energy up to the solar plexus chakra, situated above your belly button and below your chest. Breathe in golden yellow. As you breathe in the colour yellow, see your chakra become balanced with a yellow hue. If you see any muddiness or imbalance, breathe it away.

When you are ready, take the energy up to the heart chakra, situated in the chest. Visualise it in a bright green and see it expanding in loving radiance. As you breathe in the colour green, see your chakra become balanced with a green hue. If you see any muddiness or imbalance, breathe it away.

Next, take the energy up to the throat chakra, situated in the throat. Breathe in the colour blue, a bright blue. As you breathe in the colour blue, see your chakra become balanced with a blue hue. If you see any muddiness or imbalance, breathe it away.

Now take the energy up to the third eye chakra, situated on the bridge of your nose. Breathe in the colour indigo. As you breathe in the colour indigo, see your chakra become balanced with an indigo hue. If you see any muddiness or imbalance, breathe it away.

Move your attention now to the top of your head, where the crown chakra is situated. Breathe in the colour violet. As you breathe in the colour violet, see your chakra become balanced with a violet hue. If you see any muddiness or imbalance, breathe it away.

Now sit for a few moments as you feel all your chakras balanced and aligned.

When you are ready to finish, breathe each chakra back in turn, still retaining its assigned colour.

Start with the crown chakra. Breathe and see it return to its normal size, balanced and aligned.

Then move to the third eye chakra. Breathe and see it return to its normal size, balanced and aligned.

Then move to the throat chakra. Breathe and see it return to its normal size, balanced and aligned.

Then move to the heart chakra. Breathe and see it return to its normal size, balanced and aligned.

Then move to the solar plexus chakra. Breathe and see it return to its normal size, balanced and aligned.

Then move to the sacral chakra. Breathe and see it return to its normal size, balanced and aligned.

Then finally move to the base chakra. Breathe and see it return to its normal size, balanced and aligned.

Feel your whole body healthy, balanced, aligned and refreshed. Open your eyes when you are ready. Stretch and touch your feet to ground yourself.

Appendix 18

Chakra Energy Centre Meditation

This develops further on the previous chakra colour meditation.

Sit with your feet and arms uncrossed, with your feet firmly connected to the floor (you may wish to put a cushion or something similar under your feet so that they are connected to the floor).

Close your eyes. Take a few long, slow deep breaths. Be still.

Now see a pure crystalline light descend from the cosmos until it settles just above your head. It is a light of pure radiance, peace and tranquillity. It is light and it is love.

Feel the peace descend all around you and illuminate the radiance from within. You are a divine light, a spark of that divine radiance.

Begin to breathe in the white light now.

Breathe in the white light through the top of your head as it takes away all your cares and worries, stilling the mind. See all your troubles and thoughts just melt away. Be of peace. You are connecting with the wisdom of the divine higher knowledge and guidance.

Take the white light now down into your third eye, just above the bridge of your nose between the eyebrows. It gives you clear inner vision of mind, of body and of soul.

You see with clarity of vision, physically and through your mind's eye.

Now take the white light into the throat area. If the need arises, clear your throat and do so without hesitation.

Here the white light clears the throat area for clear communication, creativity and listening.

See the white light now move into the heart area. See this area expand with a deep sense of love and compassion – love for yourself and for all beings. Feel and sense the love expanding with radiance.

Move the white light now to the solar plexus area, the centre of the body, just below the ribcage. See the white light remove anxiety, worry and stress. Feel yourself centred, calm and empowered.

Next move the white light to the sacral centre, just above the pubis. See the white light clear away any feelings of guilt or shame. Feel the light connect with procreation, sexuality and creativity.

Next move the white light to the base, the perineum, the seat on which you sit. Feel the white light remove any insecurities or worries about the future. It gives stability and strength, setting firm foundations.

Now see the white light travel down your legs through the soles of your feet and into the earth as if you have roots, like the roots of trees coming from your feet, anchoring you firmly to the earth. See the white light taking away all negative energies, away from your body and into the earth to be transmuted into positive energy.

Now take a breath and breathe the light in a circular motion from your feet, up the back of your body over the front of your body and down over the front of your body the back of your body. Breathe it down into your feet.

Breathe in this circular motion up over the front and down the rear of your body and down the front three times.

Now breathe the white light up the left side of your body from your feet to the top of your head, and down the right side of your body to your feet. Breathe in this circular motion up the left and down the right side of your body three times.

Now we are going to stay here for a minute or maybe longer, enjoying the peaceful energies.

Wait for at least a minute to elapse, longer if you can.

Now it is time to come back into full alertness and awake on the count of three.

One… Coming back to full alertness.

Two… Feeling happy, peaceful and relaxed.

Three… Open your eyes, fully awake and alert.

Stretch and touch your feet if you can.

Record any experiences in your journal.

Appendix 19

Pranic Breathing

Prana is the life-giving breath, according to ancient Hindu texts. In other traditions it is known as chi or qi. It is considered to be the life force energy that is circulated around the body.

Sit comfortably, with your back upright and your feet flat on the floor. Alternatively, sit comfortably on the floor, making sure your back is upright. You may even wish to sit cross-legged like a yogi. Close your eyes.

Take a deep breath in and exhale fully with a sigh, releasing all tension with the out breath. Feel yourself relax deeply and fully as you breathe, letting go of all tension in the body.

Now, focus on the breath but breathe normally. Visualise the air entering your nose as pure white light as it fills your lungs. See the air fill your lungs with a pure, radiant light.

As you breathe out, visualise the air coming out of your nostrils as black smoke, as if you are breathing out impurities from your lungs. You are exhaling all the impurities of the body and mind. Empty your lungs fully.

Now inhale slowly, without forcing, and put your full attention onto the breath. See your lungs as having three sections: lower, middle and upper. Fill the lower part of your lungs first, then the middle section, then finally the upper section.

Hold your breath for two or three seconds. Then release the breath slowly through your nostrils, expelling all the air from your lungs. Hold for two to three seconds. Then start another inhalation.

Continue to do this for five to ten breaths initially. The number of breaths can be increased with time and practice.

Appendix 20

Alternate Nostril Breathing

This practice is commonly done before or after yoga sessions and can also be done before a meditation session, or it can be done as a stand-alone exercise. It can help clear the mind, bring clarity to thoughts and aid in relaxation. This also is a form of pranic breathing.

Sit in a comfortable position with your back upright. Place both hands on your knees. Now lift your right hand up to your nose. Exhale completely.

Then, use the thumb of your right hand to close your right nostril completely.

Now, inhale fully through your left nostril. Then close your left nostril with your finger. Open your right nostril and exhale deeply. After exhaling, inhale fully with your right nostril still open. Close your nostril with your thumb. Open your left nostril and exhale through this side.

This is one cycle. Continue for up to five minutes. Always finish with exhaling through the left nostril.

Appendix 21

Guided Visualisation: Walk in Nature

Find a quiet space where you will not be disturbed. Make sure the phone is off the hook or switched off. Have paper and a pen ready to make notes at the end. You may like to light a candle and/or burn incense.

Sit or lie comfortably and close your eyes. Begin to take nice deep breaths.

As you breathe in, imagine breathing in peace. On the out breath breathe away all tension and anxiety. Breathe in peace and love. Breathe out all tension, stresses and strains. As you breathe in, imagine all the tensions of the day and any thoughts and fears melting away with the out breath. As you breathe in again, breathe a white light through the top of your head and into your body. This white light will clear away all stresses, strains and worries. As you breathe out, imagine all these stresses, strains and worries leaving your body. Breathe in and out this way until you feel relaxed and at peace.

See roots like the roots of a tree coming out of the soles of your feet. These roots go deep, deep into the earth, grounding you so you are ready for your journey.

See a tunnel ahead of you. As you enter this tunnel you feel no fear. The tunnel is dimly lit. At the end of the tunnel you see a bright light. You head towards this bright light at the end of the tunnel.

As you emerge out of the tunnel you find yourself in field of long grass. The sun is gently shining. It's warm, not too hot. You walk through the field, feeling the softness of the earth and the grass beneath your feet. You feel the long grass with your hand as you continue walking. You smell the fresh, clean air and feel the sun shining on your face. You feel a gentle breeze in the air. You hear the birds singing in the distance. There are beautiful flowers all around in various colours. Perhaps you can see birds or other animals. Have no fear. Nothing can harm you. Everything is peaceful.

You pass by a stream, gently gurgling to your right. You stop for a moment and listen to the gentle sound of the water passing over the rocks and stones.

Ahead of you is a hill with gentle grassy slopes reaching upwards. You walk up this hill with ease. As you get to the top you see a lovely patch of grass to sit on. It looks so comfortable. This place feels so peaceful and loving. You make your way to the patch of grass and sit. The grass is lush, green and soft. As you look all around there are mountains visible in the distance. It is a beautiful place and you are overjoyed at the beauty and the peace that you are experiencing.

You sit here for a few moments, enjoying the peace and tranquillity. You may hear nature sounds or smell beautiful aromas in the air. Take time to enjoy this peaceful time. Stay here for a while.

Pause for a few minutes.

The time has come for you to end your journey. You are very grateful for this experience. You know that you can come back to this place any time you wish.

You get up from the patch of grass where you are sitting and make your way down the gentle grassy slope of the hill. You reach the field and make your way through it, feeling the grass beneath your feet. You run your hands through the grass as you go. You pass the stream, which is now to your left. You take one last look at the scenery all around you.

You see the tunnel and enter it. It is still dimly lit and you can see the light at the end. You emerge out of the tunnel to find yourself back in your quiet place. You come back into yourself.

Breathe deeply and bring yourself back to full awareness. Wriggle your toes and fingers. Run your hands down your legs and, if you can, touch your feet to ground yourself. Stretch if you want to.

Open your eyes when you are ready.

Get your paper and pen and write down everything you can remember.

References and Further Reading

Bergland, C., (2015), 'Alpha Brain Waves Boost Creativity and Reduce Depression', *Psychology Today*, published 17 April 2015, accessed online 2 June 2019.

Black, A., (2015), *The Little Pocket Book of Mindfulness,* CICO Books, London, England.

Chiba, F., (2018), *Kakeibo: The Japanese Art of Saving Money*, TarcherPerigee, USA.

Covey, S.R., (2004), *The 7 Habits of Highly Effective People: Powerful Lessons in Personal Change*, Simon & Schuster, London.

Dispenza, J., Dr, (2017), *Becoming Supernatural: How Common People Are Doing the Uncommon*, Hay House, UK.

Dyer, W., Dr, (2010), *The Power of Intention*, Hay House, USA.

Elrod, H., (2019), *The Miracle Equation*, John Murray Learning, London, England.

Elrod, H., Petrini, P., (2015), *The Miracle Morning for Network Marketers*, Hal Elrod International, USA.

Gilbert, A (1), Epel, E (1), Tanzi, R (2), Rearden, R (1), Schilf, S (1), Puterman, E (1), (2014), 'A Randomized Trial

Comparing a Brief Meditation Retreat to a Vacation: Effects on Daily Well-Being', (1) University of California, San Francisco, CA, USA, (2) Harvard University, Charlestown, MA, USA. Taken from the *Journal of Alternative and Complementary Medicine* May 2014, accessed online 30 June 2019.

Harrold, G., (2019), *De-Stress Your Life*, Orion Publishing, London, England.

Howarth Tomlinson, T., (2018), *Walking into the Light: A Seeker's Guide to Spiritual Development*, 2QT, UK.

Howarth Tomlinson, T., (2018), *Mighty Angels By Your Side*, 2QT, UK.

Mata, D., Sri, (2014), *Finding the Joy Within You: Personal Counsel for God-Centred Living*, Self-Realization Fellowship, USA.

Murphy, J., Dr, (1993), *The Power of Your Subconscious Mind*, Simon & Schuster Ltd, London, England.

Peale, N. V., (2016), *Discovering the Power of Positive Thinking*, Orient Paperbacks, New Delhi.

Shucman, H., (2007), *A Course in Miracles, (Combined Volume)*, Foundation for Inner Peace, USA

Tolle, E., (2009), *A New Earth: Create a Better Life*, Penguin, London, England.

Williams, M., Penman, D., (2011), *Mindfulness: A Practical Guide to Finding Peace in a Frantic World*, Piatkus, UK.

www.ingramcontent.com/pod-product-compliance
Lightning Source LLC
Chambersburg PA
CBHW071617080526
44588CB00010B/1160